UNDERSTANDING
YOUR DOG

Foreword by Konrad Lorenz

UNDERSTANDING
YOUR DOG

by Peter Messent

STEIN AND DAY / Publishers / New York

Title page Master of all he surveys, this magnificent dog is a Vizla, or Hungarian 'Yellow Pointer'. Developed on the central Hungarian plain, the Vizla became a multi-purpose gun dog used for tracking, pointing and retrieving game from the water.

First published in the United States of America in 1983
Copyright © 1979 by Quarto Limited
All rights reserved
Printed in the United States of America
Stein and Day/*Publishers*
Scarborough House
Briarcliff Manor, N.Y. 10510

Library of Congress Cataloging in Publication Data

Messent, Peter.
    Understanding your dog.

    Includes index.
    1. Dogs — Behavior.   2. Dogs — Training.
3. Dogs.   I.   Title.
SF433.M47   1980   636.7   80-51643
ISBN 0-8128-2746-5

Contents

Foreword

The central aim of this book, though not stated in so many words, is to promote a natural and happy relationship between Man and Dog, and to give potential dog-owners an insight into the 'language of dogs', that is, their non-verbal code of communication.

The author, a scientist with a profound knowledge of dogs, deals extensively with the manner in which different breeds have diverged from their wild ancestors as a result of selective breeding by man. In this particular respect, the book contains a great amount of important information, with a section on working dogs and the ways in which they serve man.

He shows the reader in a simple and understandable way how the different senses work in the dog. The author proves exceedingly able to 'visualize' the world of a creature whose main sensory organs are the nose and the ear, a world which is extremely different from the predominantly visual one in which we live.

Peter Messent, an ethologist, gives a very clear picture of the innate, instinctive abilities of dogs. With scientific objectivity, he informs the reader of the ineradicable traits a dog-owner must contend with, and goes on to emphasize that the greatest value of a dog is the love it can give to its master. His disquisition on the different breeds will prove valuable to prospective dog-owners in helping to decide which sort of puppy will best suit them.

One of the most valuable sections of the book, in my opinion, is the one dealing with the 'socialization' of a puppy, necessary to make it fit harmoniously into a human household and, reciprocally, of teaching a human family to live happily with a dog. Peter Messent makes it perfectly clear that he considers a human family incomplete without a dog or, even better, some dogs. However, he does not make a secret either of the difficulties encountered and of the many unfortunate ways in which the harmonious relationship may break up. He gives excellent instructions concerning the practical exigencies of bringing up a puppy, and deals in great detail with the typical mistakes committed again and again by dog-owners. He stresses with commendable vigour the fact that reward as well as punishment only takes effect when administered immediately after the desired or undesired action of the dog. So very few people realize that punishing a truant dog when it comes back from an illicit hunt does not have the effect of discouraging hunting, but of coming back openly. Many of the subtle methods of conditioning a dog have been new to me, though I have never been without a dog for the last sixty-five years.

Mutual understanding between man and dog is the most important prerequisite for founding a harmonious relationship between both. Peter Messent regards this understanding as so important, that he chooses the title of his book accordingly. The sign language of a dog is described and discussed most thoroughly and all present and prospective dog-owners should read it with the greatest attention. Every observant dog-owner has time and again been surprised by the dog's ability to judge his intentions by infinitesimal signs which the master has given quite unconsciously. The well-known phenomena of 'talking' and 'calculating' dogs are all the consequence of the dog's ability to evaluate minute, unintentionally-given signs.

As regards human education, I consider it highly important to teach children at an early age that there are other sensient creatures in the world besides human beings. All my own children have been brought up in a house teeming with dogs and all of them at a later age have proved to be dog-lovers.

Stressing the emotional value of dogs does not prevent the author from dealing very thoroughly with all the considerations of keeping a dog. The question of feeding is discussed in detail, the sermon against starchy foods and overfeeding is well worth heeding. It is a fact that dogs fed on kitchen scraps are, on average, fatter than those for which commercial dog food, tinned or otherwise prepared, is bought. It ought to be realized by all dog-owners that obesity shortens a dog's life quite considerably, a life which is much too short anyhow.

Perhaps the most important advice Peter Messent gives us concerns what to do when a dog dies. 'There is sorrow enough in the natural way, when it comes to burying Christian clay', says Rudyard Kipling, the great poet of the dog; he bids us beware of 'giving our heart to a dog to tear'. Indeed, the death of a family dog causes hardly less grief than that of a human family member and it is quite predictable that it will overpower us when 'fourteen years that nature permits, are ending in asthma or tumour or fits'. I know people who, having experienced this sorrow once, swear that they will never acquire a dog again. However, a deceased dog is more easily replaced than a person, and whoever follows Peter Messent's advice to buy a puppy at once on the old dog's death, will be able to find himself able to transfer his love for the dead dog to the living one and thus find a measure of consolation.

Prof. Dr. Konrad Lorenz.

Origins of the family of dog

Although a mystery still surrounds its origin, the dog was probably the first animal to be domesticated. Over the years, since the first taming of the wolf and the use of dogs for hunting, a close relationship has evolved between dogs and man. Today, the dog is not only a workmate, but friend, companion and part of the family.

Left The wolf, *Canis lupus*, is thought by many to be the ancestor of the domestic dog. It may look fierce, but in reality it is a shy species, avoiding man whenever possible.

The family of dog

The pet dog is known by scientists as *Canis familiaris*, and as such it is classified together with 35 other species in the family *Canidae*. Well-known members of this family include the wolf, coyote, jackal, fox and cape hunting dog. As a family, the *Canidae* are found in the wild on all continents with the exception of Antarctica. In Australia, the sole representative is the dingo, which was introduced by man relatively recently, but now lives wild.

Canid species live in a wide range of habitats, from the Sahara desert which is the home of the fennec fox, a small creature with large bat-like ears, to the cold northern wastes where the arctic fox is found. Because of its attachment to man, the domestic dog is distributed more widely than any of its wild relations. However, after thousands of years of domestication, it is now highly dependent on man for food and shelter.

The closest relatives of the domestic dog are the coyote, four species of jackal and the two species of wolf, the common or grey wolf and the red wolf which is found only in Texas and Louisiana in the United States.

Wolves were once found across all the temperate and sub-arctic areas of the northern hemisphere. Their distribution is now considerably reduced; they disappeared from the British Isles in the Middle Ages, and from much of Europe and North America during the present century. Nevertheless, the wolf figures in the folklore and legend of the many countries which it once inhabited, and it is generally reputed to be an animal to be feared. However, recent studies of wolf behaviour suggest that for centuries the animal has been a victim of irrational prejudice. It is, in fact, a highly social, co-operative hunter, which usually feeds on large game animals.

The cape hunting dog and the dhole, or Asiatic wild dog, hunt in packs and are therefore able to kill prey considerably larger than themselves. The other members of the *Canidae* sometimes may hunt in pairs or, like the coyote and some species of jackal, in families.

Distribution of the most familiar species

Coyote or prairie wolf, *Canis latrans.* New world equivalent of jackal, but more predator than scavenger.

South American Bush Dog, *Spethos venaticus.* Small species, un-dog-like in appearance.

Genera dusicyon

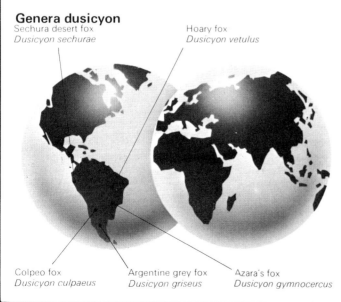

Sechura desert fox
Dusicyon sechurae

Hoary fox
Dusicyon vetulus

Colpeo fox
Dusicyon culpaeus

Argentine grey fox
Dusicyon griseus

Azara's fox
Dusicyon gymnocercus

Genera canis

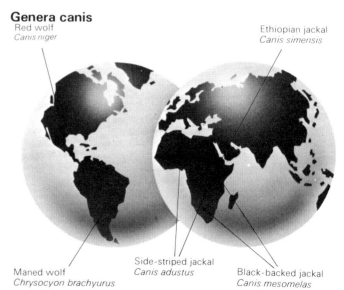

Red wolf
Canis niger

Ethiopian jackal
Canis simensis

Maned wolf
Chrysocyon brachyurus

Side-striped jackal
Canis adustus

Black-backed jackal
Canis mesomelas

The distribution of the Red Fox and Wolf is broadly similar. **Red fox**, *Vulpes vulpes*. Most widely distributed species of wild canid. Solitary by nature, has adapted well to man's presence. **Wolf**, *Canis lupus*. Now thinly distributed over its former range, extinct in some parts. Many different subspecies which vary greatly in appearance.

Arctic fox, *Alopeix lagopus*. Replaces red fox in far north. Dark summer coat turns white in winter.

Golden jackal, *Canis aureus*. Northernmost species of jackal, found in N. Africa and Middle East. As the god Anubis, revered by Egyptians.

Dhole, *Cuon alpinus*. Hunts in packs. Lives in forest areas, its history not fully known.

Cape Hunting Dog, *Lycaon pictus*. Hunts in packs like the wolf. Found in range of habitats in Africa.

Genera vulpes

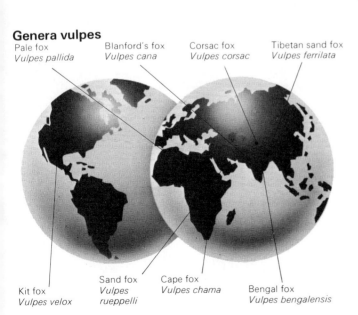

Pale fox
Vulpes pallida

Blanford's fox
Vulpes cana

Corsac fox
Vulpes corsac

Tibetan sand fox
Vulpes ferrilata

Kit fox
Vulpes velox

Sand fox
Vulpes rueppelli

Cape fox
Vulpes chama

Bengal fox
Vulpes bengalensis

Other Canidae Genera

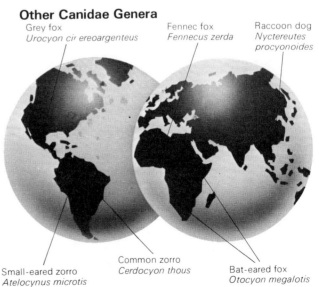

Grey fox
Urocyon cir ereoargenteus

Fennec fox
Fennecus zerda

Raccoon dog
Nyctereutes procyonoides

Small-eared zorro
Atelocynus microtis

Common zorro
Cerdocyon thous

Bat-eared fox
Otocyon megalotis

The most likely ancestor

Although the dog is man's best friend, and as such the subject of much observation and scientific study, a great mystery still surrounds his origin. This is largely because the dog was domesticated at least 12,000 years ago, and some authorities put it at even longer ago than that, at 15,000 years or more. In fact the dog was probably the first species to be domesticated, although the pig, duck, reindeer, sheep and goat are other contenders for this distinction.

Charles Darwin, the founder of modern evolutionary theory, suggested that the dog was descended from more than one species of wild canid, putting forward the wolf, coyote and various species of jackal among others. A modification of this theory was put forward by the eminent living zoologist Konrad Lorenz, who suggested that some breeds, such as chow and husky, derive from the wolf, while the majority of breeds evolved from the golden jackal. Lorenz has now altered this view; he still considers that the dog has a multiple origin, but that its ancestors are simply the different races of wolf, which are indeed quite different from one another in size and colour.

Another major problem in determining with any certainty the ancestor, or ancestors, of the dog is that there are few significant differences in terms of anatomy, behaviour or genetics between many of the canid species. Indeed it has been found that in certain circumstances the wolf, coyote and jackal will breed with each other and with the domestic dog. Moreover, the resultant offspring are

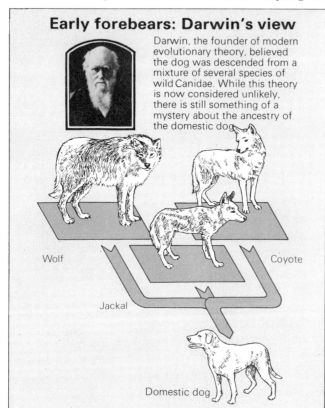

Early forebears: Darwin's view

Darwin, the founder of modern evolutionary theory, believed the dog was descended from a mixture of several species of wild Canidae. While this theory is now considered unlikely, there is still something of a mystery about the ancestry of the domestic dog.

Wolf

Coyote

Jackal

Domestic dog

Below The grey or timber wolf which once ranged extensively throughout Europe. The wolf is considered to be the most likely ancestor of the dog, being a highly social animal. Recent attempts to tame wolves suggest that a docile strain could be developed.

generally fertile, unlike the mule which is the result of a liaison between a horse and a donkey. This is not surprising in the light of the fact that the chromosomes in the cells of all these species appear to be almost identical when examined under a microscope.

A strong argument in favour of the wolf as the dog's ancestor is that, like the domestic dog but unlike the jackal or coyote, it is a highly social animal. However, the debate goes on and will doubtless continue for many years. In 1977 the zoologist Bouquegneau argued that the jackal will display dog-like social behaviour in certain circumstances and should therefore be considered a possible ancestor of the domestic dog.

A quite different suggestion, for which there is little evidence at present, is that there was a dingo-like dog living in Europe and Asia in prehistoric times and that the domestic dog is derived from this.

The mystery of the dog's origin remains, but at present, by majority consent, the wolf is considered the most likely ancestor. However, it is likely that the domestic dog has interbred with different races of wolf and perhaps with the jackal at various times, and that this has produced some of the variations seen in the domestic dog. The huge variations between breeds can also be explained by the theory that the dog was domesticated in several parts of the world at around the same time; different peoples practised selective breeding with these early domestic dogs, but with very different ends in mind.

The likely lineage

The wolf has nearly forty recognized races. The four shown on this map represent those which have been most often reported as likely later ancestors of the domestic dog, with some mixing of the races.

Canis lycaon

Canis lupus

Canis pallipes

Canis lupus chanco

Domestic dog

The dog in ancient times

Left A typical statue of the Egyptian god Anubis, jackal-headed god of death. The city of Cynopolis, the City of the Dog, was built in his honour.

Below The god Anubis in the form of a jackal, with a priest worshipping at his feet.

Right Detail of the Assyrian bas-relief of Asshurbanipal showing wild asses being hunted by dogs, which appear to be a type of mastiff. Cuneiform inscriptions enable us to trace these dogs back to 2000 BC.

Once the wolf had been tamed, specialist breeds of what was by then a dog seem to have developed quite quickly. Egyptian pottery, 7500 years old, shows a dog of the Greyhound/Saluki type which had almost certainly been bred to chase game in the desert. Greyhounds and Salukis therefore have the longest known pedigrees of all modern breeds, although they have undoubtedly changed since their early days in the desert.

All the evidence suggests that the ancient Egyptians cared as much for their dogs as most modern civilizations, if not more so. Many of their towns had special dog graveyards, and Anubis, the jackal-headed god of death was the object of devout worship and reverence.

Frescoes, bronzes, carvings and written references re-

veal that by 2000 BC the Egyptians had mastered the principles of breeding and developed it to a high level of sophistication; several breeds are depicted, and these include a toy dog, similar to a Maltese, bred almost certainly as a pet and not for any practical purpose.

Sculptures from Babylon, which date from around 2000 BC, show dogs very similar to modern Mastiffs. It seems these were trained to fight in battle, as well as being used for hunting. It is likely that, at a given command from their handlers, they would run ahead and attack the enemy. The use of dogs in this way spread later on to Europe, and even to England, where it is reported that dogs were used against the invading Romans in 55 BC.

The use of dogs for domestic purposes, such as herding

Dogs featured in the mythology and daily life of the Greeks.
Left Vase painting depicting Actaeon the hunter who was turned into a stag by Artemis, and devoured by his own dogs.
Below A lamp in the form of a Greyhound's head, holding the head of a hare in its mouth.

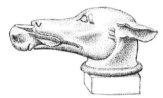

Below left A Roman statue of the Egyptian god Anubis, whom the Romans also worshipped. They made sacrifices to him, believing that he conducted the souls of the dead to the Underworld.
Below right The Romans kept many types of dogs – for guarding, herding and hunting, as well as ferocious war dogs.

Below A Roman funeral urn. The carving shows the dying man surrounded by mourners and a faithful dog is very much part of the group.

and guarding, is not so well documented. Peaceful activities of this kind are not represented as frequently in ancient art as religious ritual, war and hunting. However, it is certain that dogs for these purposes have been bred in Europe and elsewhere for several thousand years. Certainly the Romans had separate descriptive names for house dogs, shepherd dogs, sporting dogs, war dogs, dogs which would fight in arenas as a spectacle, dogs which hunted by scent, and those which hunted by sight. Some of these dogs had specific names which related to regions of the Roman Empire.

The Malamute, the sled and guard dog of the North American Eskimos, was present when Europeans first reached America. It is thought that they have remained

close to their present form for several thousand years.

Some of the dogs depicted by Egyptian artists appear to be pet dogs. However, definite evidence of selective breeding for pets dates from a few hundred years BC in Greece. Again, these appear to be of the Maltese type and they were obviously widespread, since similar dogs are reported in Rome a few hundred years later.

Quite separately, the Chinese developed their own famous breed of pet dog, the Pekingese. These miniature dogs were bred during the T'ang dynasty, beginning in the 7th century AD, and were closely associated with the ruling emperors. Pekingeses were also called lion dogs, because the objective was to breed them to look as much like miniature lions as possible.

The taming of the wolf

As discussed in the section on the dog's most likely ancestor, its origins date from its domestication at least 12,000 years ago, some authorities even say 15,000. This suggests that the dog was the first species to be domesticated, before the pig, duck, reindeer, sheep or goat. The recent discovery in Israel of a man's skeleton buried with his hand resting on a 4- to 5-month old puppy. This indicates that there was already an affectionate relationship between the two and the dog's teeth indicate that it had already undergone some domestication.

The geographical spread of fossil sites, and the distribution of certain breeds across the world today, suggest that domestication almost certainly took place at a number of different times and places. If dogs are descended from wolves, as seems likely, it is easy to see how this happened.

Man would have lived close to wolves in most parts of the world, and if early man was anything like modern man, it is probable that stray wolf cubs were brought home and looked after by children and their mothers. After all, stray badgers, foxes, deer and other wild species are frequently reared and kept as household pets today.

Attempts have been made to tame wolves in recent years, and these have shown that they are much less docile than dogs and more fearful of anything unfamiliar. However, not all wolves are the same, some being more amenable and well disposed towards humans than others. If wolves of favourable temperament had been selectively bred, a strain of tame wolves could have been established very quickly.

A group of Russians have done just this very recently with silver foxes. The tamest individuals from a group were bred with each other over about twelve generations; the resulting foxes were just as tame as domestic dogs, and quite unlike their wild counterparts.

Clearly then, the offspring of abandoned wolf cubs could

have become pet wolves over a small number of generations; but there is an argument against this theory of the dog's origin. Not only would a pet wolf have offered no economic benefit to his masters, but, as a carnivore, he would have eaten a significant quantity of scarce food.

It has to be assumed that the pet wolf began to earn his keep very quickly. He may well have been useful as a guard, alerting his masters to the approach of dangerous animals, or indeed humans. He may have been used as a work animal, pulling sledges for example, and his skin would almost certainly have provided clothing. Other functions could have quickly evolved: guarding flocks; catching game; tracking and flushing out prey using his superior sense of smell.

The long association between man and his best friend must have started in some such way as this. But why, of all the carnivorous species that he might have tamed, did man choose only the wolf and much later the Kaffir cat of the Middle East? In the case of the wolf the answer must lie in the social nature of this animal in the wild.

By selecting the tamest wolves and rearing them with humans from puppyhood, the social dependence of the wolf on other members of the pack, especially the head wolf, could easily have been transferred to man. Treating man as the pack leader, the domestic wolf would have given him total obedience and support, the very qualities which have long endeared the dog to man.

In the past, the wolf has been regarded as an animal to fear – the villain of the Red Riding Hood story, the horrifying werewolf. However, it is also reputed to have adopted human babies lost in the wild as in the legend of Romulus and Remus, **above**. Today, the more benevolent reputation seems the truer one.

The Australian Wild Dog or Dingo

Shaded area shows distribution of the dingo

Perth
Adelaide
Sydney
Melbourne

The dingo is found only in Australia and is an enigma of the dog family. It is a wild animal preying on small marsupials, sheep and chickens and other domestic animals, and yet it is so like the domestic dog in every other way that it is classified as the same species. This makes it the only wild member of *Canis familiaris*.

Apart from man, the dingo is the only large indigenous non-marsupial carnivorous mammal on the Australian continent, and it is generally agreed that it must have been brought there by man – probably about 9000 years ago.

One theory is that the dingo was then a domesticated pet and has since gone wild. However, some zoologists maintain that the dingo is so hard to tame that it can never have been a domestic dog. If this is so, it would appear that, for some reason known only to themselves, early voyagers to Australia chose to bring a wild animal with them.

On balance it seems more likely that many thousands of years ago the dingo was a domesticated pet; the Pariah dogs of Asia might then be his tame descendants, but in Australia he reverted to the wild and has survived only in this form.

Below left and right Russian children playing with wolf cubs. The image of the wolf as a ferocious and threatening animal is changing today, as studies using methods such as attaching radio transmitters to wolves, show that they are shy of people, and are highly social, co-operative hunters.

Man's best friend

Unlike the cat, which is a natural loner, the dog is by nature a gregarious, friendly animal. As has been seen, the first dogs were very probably descended from tamed wolf cubs, the offspring of social animals who lived in packs. In the absence of the pack these early predecessors of the modern dog gave the allegiance and affection, which is a part of their nature, to the humans who reared them. A dog's friends became his human companions, who were themselves social animals, happy to reciprocate the gestures of friendship made towards them.

And so it has been ever since. The first dogs helped man in many ways – guarding, herding, fighting and hunting – but, that man saw the dog as something more than just economically useful was revealed early on when he chose to breed dogs specifically as pets. What is a pet, but a friend?

Of course, many dogs still perform a working role as well as providing friendship, but it is significant that in a recent survey 88 per cent of dog owners gave companionship as a reason for keeping their dogs. A much smaller number, 40 per cent, mentioned the protection that the dog afforded them.

In most countries, the numbers of dogs kept as pets has grown dramatically over the last 50 years. Even remotely reliable figures have only been available in recent years, but the figures shown here (see table) can be taken as reasonably accurate.

The most dogs per numbers of households are found in the United States and France, where almost one family in

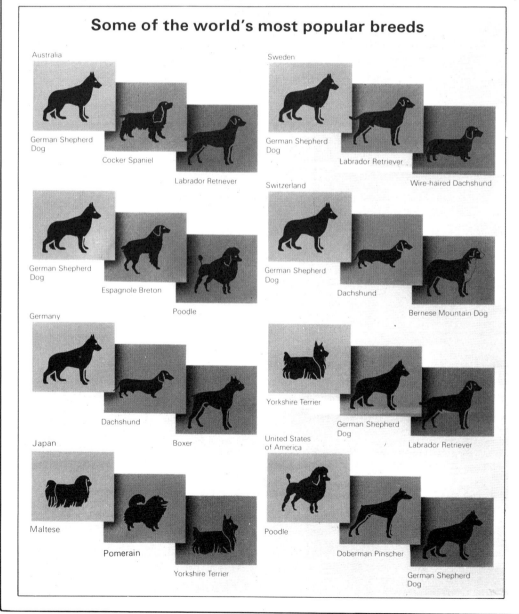

Some of the world's most popular breeds

Australia
German Shepherd Dog
Cocker Spaniel
Labrador Retriever

German Shepherd Dog
Espagnole Breton
Poodle

Germany
Dachshund
Boxer

Japan
Maltese
Pomerain
Yorkshire Terrier

Sweden
German Shepherd Dog
Labrador Retriever
Wire-haired Dachshund

Switzerland
German Shepherd Dog
Dachshund
Bernese Mountain Dog

Yorkshire Terrier
German Shepherd Dog
Labrador Retriever

United States of America
Poodle
Doberman Pinscher
German Shepherd Dog

Below This peaceful scene indicates the strong bond that exists between the dog and the elderly man. Actively seeking the companionship of humans, giving affection openly, the dog can by its very presence make life happier and easier for its owner.

three has a dog. The lowest levels of dog ownership are found in Germany and Switzerland, 11 per cent of households, and in Japan, 13 per cent. In the United Kingdom about 25 per cent of all households have a dog.

Few attempts have been made to explain the growth of dog ownership which has occurred during this century. The scientific studies and surveys that have been made, suggest that changes in the organization of society have made more people seek the companionship that a dog offers. Urban man has become separated from his relatives, and neighbourliness too has suffered as people move readily from place to place seeking better jobs, houses and so on. A man's dog, on the other hand, is always pleased to see him and ready to give and receive affection.

To most ways of thinking, a dog fulfils the role of companion or friend better than a cat, which is by nature a more independent, solitary animal. It is significant then that, in almost every country where statistics exist, dogs are now more popular than cats.

The protection offered by a dog is obviously an important factor, and here again he scores over the cat. His ability to guard his owner and his home was one of the qualities which first endeared him to man thousands of years ago. In those days he afforded protection from wild animals; now he serves to ward off human assailants and intruders.

Through history, the dog has proved remarkably adaptable, yet another quality man looks for when choosing his best friend.

The image-maker

Below left The white Borzois were chosen to enhance this filmstar's glamorous image. The Old English Sheepdog owner in the bottom picture has selected a robust pet to suit his personality, and the older woman has a friendly, comforting companion.

The dog, as friend and partner, will allow its owner to love and feel loved with none of the risks involved in human relationships. Is it surprising, then, that surveys of dog owners reveal companionship as the most common reason for keeping a dog?

Companionship has many facets, but fundamental to them all is the dog's capacity to act as a true friend, an unremitting partner who will never let his owner down whatever happens. Many people say that a dog is a better friend than any human can ever be; he seeks to please, is uncompetitive, and does not judge the owner on his or her personal qualities.

Dogs are also fond of, and encourage, physical contact between man and another living being – Western man often being conditioned to be reticent in this respect. Owners may not realize it, but stroking, cuddling, and being licked in return, can be very good for them psychologically. Babies derive comfort from close contact with their mothers, but it is often forgotten that adults can benefit in a similar way from a physical, but non-sexual, relationship.

In many western societies, overt physical contact between people in public is frowned upon, or at least most people are inhibited about it. However, in the same societies cuddling a dog is seen as nothing strange. Western man certainly practises much less touch behaviour than do the members of many other cultures and indeed any of his nearest relatives among the apes.

It is significant that recently dogs have been used with great success in certain mental hospitals. Patients who have ceased to communicate with humans have responded to approaches made by dogs, and through this have gradually regained their faith in humanity. One reason for

Dogs and their owners often look alike. The gypsy and his Lurcher, **right**, have a similar lean, alert quality, while the elderly lady and the fragile-looking Whippet are well matched. **Bottom picture** Playing on this idea, the model and the Poodle set a style.

this is that a dog is not affected by abnormality in humans, and will respond in his usual friendly way.

There are other psychological benefits to be had from a dog's companionship. A person's self-esteem – his confidence in the image he presents to the world – can be boosted by his dog. For example, some people – more than might be immediately apparent – see their dogs as an extension of themselves. An Afghan hound might be seen as sleek and attractive, while a German Shepherd dog could be considered masculine and forceful. On a less superficial level, a man with no vain pretensions, but who sees himself as a genial person, well-liked by people of all ages, might, almost sub-consciously, have a friendly, un-aggressive, rather portly mongrel as his constant companion.

Studies have shown that, as well as being an immense practical help, guide dogs raise the self-esteem of their blind owners. The guide dog owners were seen to be members of a small, high status group in the blind community, with much greater independence.

A person with a dog as a companion is often likely to make new acquaintances than someone out for a walk on their own or just with other people. The dog will not only tend to get his owner out walking in streets or parks where he might not otherwise go, but will often initiate a conversation with a stranger, either a fellow dog owner or a dog admirer. A recent survey in Sweden found that almost two-thirds of dog owners credited their dog with providing opportunities for conversation, and well over half felt that their dog had 'got them friends'. Only five per cent said that their dog had 'got them enemies' Thus a dog frequently acts as a catalyst in human relationships.

Dogs and children

A family with young children is also likely to have a pet dog, and this seems to be the case on both sides of the Atlantic. In Britain, the level of dog ownership in households with children is about double that in childless households. This may be because children persuade their parents to buy dogs, but there could be at least one other explanation: perhaps the parents consider that a dog in the home will in some way help their child's development.

This theory has been put forward by an American psychologist, Dr B. Levinson, who has made a study of the relationship between children and pets. In an age of working wives and nuclear families, Levinson argues, the dog fills a gap in the child's life. When both parents are out at work, when there are no brothers and sisters to play with, the dog acts as a companion, as well as being a useful protector. For the very young child, the dog can act as a human substitute, unlike a lifeless doll or some other toy.

Older children need outlets for imaginative play. This helps vent their tensions, frustrations, fears and hostilities. It also permits them to express their creativity. In both cases, a pet dog can be a participant in play, while also helping prevent make-believe activities from becoming too unreal, Levinson argues. Once the dog has assumed an importance in imaginative games, it will also be valued in reality. Not only will this keep the child in touch with reality, it will also help the child develop a sense of responsibility towards animals, and perhaps ultimately towards people.

The child can also be taught to help in caring for the dog, feeding it, and taking it for walks. These activities are a natural focus for discussion between the child and the parents. There will be discussions, and there will be planning, which will involve the child with the parents. In this way, the dog acts as a useful bridge between the generations and a buttress to emotional stability in the family.

The responsibility of training a dog is beneficial for the child.

While games with the dog are fun, its welfare must be safeguarded.

Left The child must learn the correct way to hold the dog, supporting its weight.
Opposite Young children growing up with a dog will have a companion, protector and playmate.

One of the family

Above The dog's place in the Greek family is indicated by this 4th-century relief in Athens.

Considered by their owners to be part of the family, dogs themselves obviously feel they have a rightful place in the family group. The dog in the 16th-century picture, **right**, is as much at home with the children as the Victorian lap dog with its mistress, **opposite right**, and the pet in the contemporary photograph.

In many countries, the keeping of a dog is seen as a way of completing a family. This can be traced back to Victorian times in England where many family portraits would include the pet dog.

Surveys have shown that the dog is not only the most common household pet, but that he gives the most satisfaction, and indeed value for money. A recent survey of pet owners made by a British consumer organization concluded that the dog was the 'best buy' among pets. He scored highest on the amount of enjoyment he gave his owners each day, somewhere in the region of four hours per family. This was well ahead of the cat, equalled only by the pet horse, which is considerably more expensive to keep.

It is difficult to compare dogs and cats as pets, because their behaviour and their role in the family are very different. This is reflected by the fact that few people class themselves as both dog and cat lovers; dog owners love dogs, and cat owners love cats, and only rarely do the two views coincide. This was established in a survey made by a group of psychologists, but they also found that both dog and cat lovers had a high level of affection for other humans. The inference is that animal lovers are more friendly towards their fellows than are those people who are indifferent to animals.

This finding ties up with the fact, mentioned on an earlier page, that families with children are twice as likely to have a dog as childless households. Clearly, the dog in some way suits, and fits into, a family group. This must have a lot to do with his wolf ancestry, and his natural preference for living in a group or pack.

Wolves live in large families with elaborate social structures and are obedient to the leaders. Dogs are quite happy to do the same, considering the leaders to be the members of the family who feed them and give them orders. The dog is not just seen by his owners as a member of the family; he sees himself as a member as well

Physique and intelligence

How well does a dog see, smell and hear? How does it differ from us in the way it uses these senses for communicating with other dogs and humans? Physique may vary greatly from breed to breed, but certain behaviour patterns are common to all: the 'play bow' used to solicit a game; the submissive pose; the aggressive face. Canine intelligence is more difficult to assess – is a clever dog intelligent or just highly-trained?

Left This German Shepherd Dog sits in a typical pose indicating alertness: ears point forward to focus any sound, eyes watch out for the slightest movement.

The thinking dog

Whether dogs and other animals think, or in other words use reason when making a decision, is a question which has bothered philosophers and scientists for centuries. After a lot of thought, the Greek philosopher Aristotle decided that although animals could learn and remember things, only humans were capable of reason.

Humans can also talk to one another using language. All animals communicate with one another in some way – vocally, visually or by some other method – but the level of communication possible with the human languages is thought by many experts to be in a class of its own. Sentence structure, vocabulary and subtle intonation can be used to communicate original thoughts which have never been expressed before.

A dog can understand a number of commands, such as sit, come, wait and heel, but it cannot understand sentences. The way dogs communicate, although there is still much to be learnt about it, seems to take the form of fairly simple signals. Only man's nearest relatives, the apes, provoke any serious argument as to whether animals possess language.

The ability to think and reason is partly related to brain size, so it is hardly surprising that the dog's mental capacity is much smaller than that of a human. For example with a dog of comparable weight, such as a St Bernard, the brain weighs 15 per cent of that of a man.

If the dog has no command of language and a much more limited mental capacity than man, does it think at all and, if so, how? It is impossible to go inside a dog's mind to see how it works, but relevant observations can be made.

It is certain that dogs dream. When they sleep, they sometimes twitch and move their eyes rapidly under closed eyelids. These are both indications of dreaming in humans, but what a dog dreams of no one knows.

There are other parallels between human and canine mental processes. There are many recorded instances of dogs showing grief at the death of their owners. Probably the most famous case was a dog called Bobby, to whom a monument has been erected in Edinburgh. Bobby followed his master's coffin to the graveyard and stayed near the tomb for the rest of his life; he survived his owner by 14 years. Was he displaying grief, or did he simply establish a new territory, feeling that this was where he belonged?

Another important question is whether dogs have special abilities which humans do not possess, a sixth sense or any kind of extra-sensory perception. There are many stories of dogs, left behind when their owners move house, finding their way to the new home several hundred miles away.

Animals may well have better powers of navigation than humans – birds certainly do – but it is a mystery how a dog knows which way to go in such instances.

Other evidence of an apparent sixth sense can be explained more easily. Some of their five known senses are attuned differently from those of humans. For example, they can detect more highly pitched notes; their sense of smell is superior; and it is possible that they can detect warmth through special receptors in their noses. This may explain some of their more unusual feats, such as detecting

Intelligence is difficult to assess in animals; there is no evidence that dogs are able to reason as man does. Dogs that learn to open doors, fetch newspapers, **right**, and perform tricks, do so as a result of training and instinct.

a bugging device from its high pitched emissions and giving early warning of a fire using their sense of smell. It may even explain how dogs have apparently predicted earthquakes by suddenly behaving in an odd way some time before the event; one theory is that dogs can smell gas seeping from the ground. Another is that they detect low frequency warning vibrations.

It is still unclear whether any of a dog's behaviour is motivated by thought. As more research is done, it may be possible to explain some of the oddities of dog behaviour, where it appears they may be thinking. Trying to make a dog understand human language does not reveal much about the dog's mind. A better approach is to discover more about how dogs communicate with each other, and even how they try to communicate with us.

Unfortunately, if it is difficult to determine whether dogs think, it is even harder to measure their intelligence. First of all, intelligence is difficult to define, even in human terms. Most people think of it as something similar to being

smart, clever, brilliant or some other word which broadly describes academic, or problem-solving, prowess. However, the following definition may help up to a point: 'the mental pattern or framework which a person or animal uses to tackle a problem, based on its physical abilities and upbringing'.

Even if a broad definition of this kind can be agreed upon, reasonable tests have to be devised. This is difficult enough for humans, and almost impossible for dogs and other animals.

Clearly, any test of intelligence must be tailored to suit a particular species; it is impossible to make more than the broadest of comparisons between species. However, even within the dog species problems arise because there are so many different breeds. To take an extreme example, a Pekingese and a Great Dane can hardly be given a test which involves jumping up to retrieve an object. Most of the breeds have special aptitudes, and this makes it almost impossible to devise a general test of dog intelligence.

This leaves the possibility of assessing intelligence merely by observing a particular dog's behaviour. Some dogs certainly perform extraordinary feats, which apparently require great intelligence. There are dogs who collect the morning newspaper from the newsagent; others can get out of a room by undoing the latch; many dogs learn strange tricks such as riding along with two or three legs on a skateboard.

Acts of this kind appear to reflect intelligence, but they must be looked at against the inbred qualities of the dogs in question, and also the behaviour of dogs in general. Some breeds of dog have been trained to retrieve objects for generations; to them the collection of a newspaper is an admittedly more complex form of a process which comes to them very easily.

A dog who opens a door with the latch is likely to have found the solution by chance, perhaps by nuzzling the latch in an attempt to push the door open, rather than by thinking the problem through.

Training or intelligence?

Dexterous   Dogs.

Several remarkable dogs have been shown to the public from time to time. One seemed to be extremely proficient at mental arithmetic – addition, subtraction and multiplication. He barked his answers – one bark for one, two barks for two and so on – and he was always correct, even on fairly difficult calculations.

However, close study of this performance revealed that the dog was not actually making calculations to produce the answers. Quite inadvertently, the owner was giving the dog a cue as to when to stop barking; he would watch the dog, anxiously waiting for each bark until the correct total was reached, then he would relax and sit back slightly. The owner was not aware that he was doing this, but the dog certainly noticed it. When he perceived this change of attitude, he would immediately stop barking.

It might be said that this dog displayed intelligence; it was certainly very sensitive to the mood of its owner but it must be recognized that dogs respond readily to body postures, this being their principal means of communicating with each other.

Dogs can be trained easily, may be intelligent, but it must be remembered that they can only be trained in areas for which they have a special aptitude; the offspring of Labradors who are champions at retrieving are unlikely to

It is very easy to confuse the capacity to respond to training with intelligence. Dogs which are trained for specific working roles – guide dogs; police dogs like the one pictured, **right**, searching for weapons in Northern Ireland; sheep dogs; circus dogs, **left**, performing tricks – are all subject to intensive training, and sometimes specific breeds respond best.

make good guide dogs, and nor are the puppies of champion sheep dogs. This shows that the breeding, or genetic background of a dog may effect its capacity to be trained.

In some cases, such as guide dogs, a planned breeding programme is used to produce a higher percentage pass rate, with more dogs successfully completing training.

Upbringing also has a major influence on a dog's behaviour. If a dog has been kept in kennels for the first four months of its life, it will probably never be fully trainable, certainly not to the extent of a puppy brought into a family at the age of six weeks. This does not mean that there is any difference in the intelligence of the two

dogs, just that their backgrounds give them a different capacity to accept training.

It is clear then that a highly trained dog is not necessarily exceptionally intelligent. Those who seek to measure a dog's level of intelligence must bear several factors in mind: the breed and size of dog; its ancestry and upbringing; whether it has had special training; whether it is a frightened individual who might otherwise behave more sensibly; whether it has discovered skills by chance and developed them by practice. Only if all these factors can be evaluated, can a proper assessment of intelligence be made.

The expressive face

Facial expressions are an important method of communication for dogs, with ears, eyes and mouth conveying a range of feelings. **Right top** Erect ears and an intense gaze indicate alertness. **Right bottom** The fearful dog. Ears are flattened and teeth bared. **Opposite top** The grin, shown only to people, is intended as a friendly greeting, and is thought to be a mimic of the human smile. **Opposite bottom** These threatening features indicate aggression: staring eyes, ears erect and teeth bared.

A dog's sense of hearing and smell are both more highly developed than his sight, but it is through visual signals that dogs communicate most, at least at close range. Some of these gestures have an obvious meaning to humans; others are generally misinterpreted because they do not mean to people what they do to a dog. Some dogs are unable to make certain gestures because breeding has so radically altered their face, body or tail.

Several parts of the face have special functions in communication. The eyes play a very important part. The direct stare of one dog at another, or of a man at a dog is one of the most potent forms of communication. The stare is a threat signal to other dogs, and is ordinarily only given by a dominant dog to a submissive one, or else as a prelude to a fight. If a person stares at a dog, the dog will generally look away and become submissive, often sitting down and rolling on its side, and even urinating, a sign of intense submission. Occasionally, a stare can provoke a retaliatory attack from a dominant dog.

The ears can convey a great deal about a dog's feelings. In general, ears that are held well back against the head

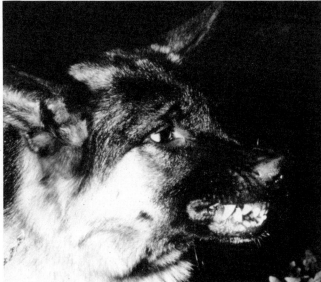

indicate either submission or fear, depending on other aspects of the dog's facial expression. Ears that are held erect indicate that the dog is alert. This again must be seen in conjunction with the rest of the dog's facial expression; it can mean either that the dog is friendly and perhaps willing to play, or that he is in an aggressive mood. While this feature can be read in many dogs, those breeds with floppy ears are in an unfortunate position in that they must convey a permanent signal of submission to other dogs, at least with their ears. Similarly, dogs with cropped erect ears must convey a continual expression of alertness.

A range of feelings are conveyed by mouth and lips, including submission, play soliciting and alertness; again this must be interpreted with other body signals.

A facial expression that has reportedly been shown by some dogs towards people, but not towards other dogs, is the grin. This has many features of the aggressive threat face, but when accompanied by tail-wagging and flattened ears, it is obviously a friendly greeting. The best explanation of this unusual expression in a dog, is that it is deliberate mimicry of the human smile.

Body language

A dog's facial expressions are generally accompanied by changes in body posture, including the way he holds his tail. When a dog is indicating either fear or aggression, he presents himself to his potential opponent looking as big as possible. In either case, he will stand erect, but if he is afraid, he will lean backwards slightly on his legs. In both cases the hairs on his shoulders and rump, known as the hackles, will be raised to increase his apparent size. Apart from the difference in facial expression already described (see p.32), the two postures differ in that the tail is held high by an aggressive dog, but low or even between the legs by a fearful one.

A dog crouching down on four legs, with tail and head down and ears held back, is showing submission. Most people see this as the dog cowering after it has been naughty. In part this is the truth, but the dog is more likely to be showing submission to the angry look of its dominant owner, rather than displaying a genuine feeling of 'I know I've done wrong'. If a dog is feeling especially submissive, he will roll over on his side to display his belly; in many breeds this is pale in colour, equivalent to showing the white flag, and this indeed is a close description of what the dog is trying to communicate.

When a dog crouches low on his front legs with his back legs raised and tail held high, he is soliciting play; he will adopt the same posture towards a human or another dog. He is likely to move his front paws up and down, and also jump about returning to this same posture, possibly even barking as well in his attempt to make someone join in.

The greeting ritual of dogs is a very familiar one. Unless aggression is involved, in which case one or both dogs will adopt the aggressive posture already described, two dogs will usually begin by sniffing each other briefly nose to nose. If the dogs are strangers, they will indicate mutual submission, by holding their tails low and their ears back, and they will avoid prolonged eye contact by looking away. Up to this point, a similar routine is adopted by a dog greeting a person, except that the dog will sniff his leg rather than his face, because the face is usually the wrong

The dog's expressive body language

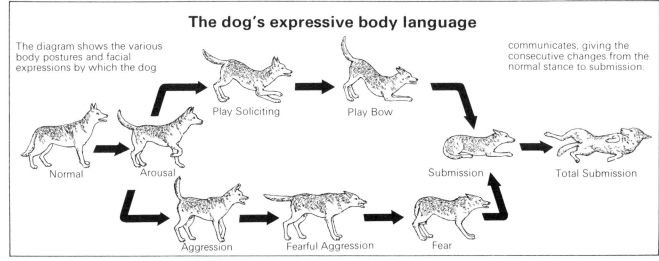

The diagram shows the various body postures and facial expressions by which the dog communicates, giving the consecutive changes from the normal stance to submission.

Normal   Arousal

Play Soliciting   Play Bow

Submission   Total Submission

Aggression   Fearful Aggression   Fear

Below right The classic ritual of strange dogs meeting–sniffing nose to nose, ears back, tail held low, indicating mutual submission.
Below Left The small dog rolls over to show its belly to the larger one. **Bottom right** The pose of a submissive dog responding to its owner's angry look.

height. Particularly if the person or the other dog is well known, he will also wag his tail vigorously from the start.

When dog meets dog, the next stage is usually a mutual investigation of the inguinal region; this is a sign of submission on both sides, similar in meaning to a dog rolling on his side. This type of contact is not normally made by a human, but in the show ring some handlers touch their dogs in this area to reassure them and calm them down.

As has been seen, the tail plays an important part in the dog's body language. Several breeds have problems here, because they have been bred to have curly tails, short tails, tails held high or low, or even no tails at all – the result of docking. How much this confuses other dogs, is uncertain, but the wagging of a dog's tail can still be seen even in dogs with the shortest of tails. This means, of course, that the dog is excited or wants to play.

The playful dog

The dog is an exceptionally playful animal and this characteristic seems to have been encouraged by man over the years of domestication. Dogs play in innumerable ways and they use a whole range of postures and routines in their attempts to initiate play with others.

The classic play soliciting pose is head down and front legs bent with back legs and tail up; this is sometimes called the play bow and has been analyzed in detail by Marc Bekoff of Colorado University. He found that, when used to initiate play, the play bow was remarkably constant in duration and highly stereotyped in performance. This suggests that it is used as a signal to other dogs announcing that what follows is intended as play, rather than, say, aggressive behaviour. This is a classic example of the dog's language, and one which can be seen in every pet dog. The play bow is also used during play itself, perhaps to reiterate the intention of continuing the game.

Although the play bow is the commonest signal used to initiate play, there are several other approaches a dog may use. One classic ploy is to tempt another dog or person, usually with an object like a ball or a stick. The dog may start to run off with the toy hoping to be chased by another dog. Alternatively the dog may drop the object completely, giving the other dog or human a chance – probably a small one – to grab it. This may happen repeatedly, and then, when he has won enough times, the dog will let his opponent grab the object and start a chasing game. Panting during the tempting game probably indicates this is play.

The dog may assume different poses during the course of the game, from the classic bow soliciting play to others indicating submission.

To initiate play with a smaller dog, the naturally dominant larger one will often roll on his back, assuming a submissive posture.

Tugging the other dog's tail to elicit a playful response.

Tempting behaviour: the opponent is offered the ball.

To indicate playful rather than aggressive behaviour, the dog will adopt what is known as the 'play bow' posture: hindquarters and tail held high, front part of the body crouching. This is one of the classic examples of the dog's body language.

An important aspect of play is that the normal dominance relationships between dogs cease to be observed. This is almost certainly why a large dog, trying to persuade a smaller dog to play, will frequently fall down on its back in front of the small dog. This is a submissive posture as well as an invitation to play, and it therefore indicates to the smaller dog that what follows is play, not in earnest.

When all else has failed, there are other manoeuvres which dogs may attempt in order to persuade one another to play. One of these is biting or tugging on the tail which may, however, elicit an aggressive rather than a playful response. Alternatively, a dog may make exaggerated movements to try and attract attention. These may include great leaps in the air, or bounding forwards and backwards, or from side to side. The bounding from side to side involves exposure of the flank to the potential play partner. This is another example of the dog indicating that he is not being aggressive.

Although tail wagging is often seen both before and during play, it is probably not a play signal as such. As described elsewhere, tail wagging seems primarily to indicate a general state of excitement rather than any particular desire or need.

The inside story

All dogs, even the St. Bernard and the Chihuahua, have broadly similar skeletal structures. They all have the same number of bones, and these are of reasonably uniform shape throughout the species. However, centuries of selective breeding have caused the relative lengths of bones to vary immensely from one breed to another. For example, the Scotch Terrier has very short limb bones and a relatively large head, while the Greyhound has very long limb bones and a relatively small skull and body skeleton.

A dog's nails, or claws, are the equivalent of human finger and toe-nails, but they are much stronger. Dogs are not good at climbing in part because their claws are not retractile like a cat's. Also, a dog's skeleton has essentially evolved for running long distances over fairly flat terrain. A cat's skeleton, on the other hand, is highly flexible enabling it to turn its whole body and limbs for gripping while climbing, but it is not suited for running in more than short bursts.

A dog's tail performs a different function from that of a cat, which is used largely to help the cat balance as well as for communication. The different breeds of dogs have tails of all shapes and sizes, but they make a limited contribution to the dog's sense of balance. The tail is used primarily for communication; wagging it, letting it droop, and moving it in a variety of ways enables the dog to express his feeling to both humans and other dogs.

Every breed of dog has the same number of the four different types of teeth – incisors, canines, premolars and molars. The dog's own scientific name is used to describe the pair of large tearing teeth, seen at top and bottom towards the front of a dog's mouth; these are, of course, found in other species including man.

The bite of the incisors at the front of the mouth varies between the breeds. A level bite is when the six top and bottom incisors meet evenly; if they overlap slightly, this is known as a scissor bite. An undershot bite is where the lower jaw protrudes beyond the upper one, while an overshot bite is the opposite condition.

These jaw differences are caused by the structure of the skull, a part of the dog which has been subject to strong selective breeding. Like the skeleton, there are fundamental similarities between the skulls of all dogs, but selection has produced great variation, from, for example, the very flat face of the Pekingese to the long face of the Borzoi.

Skulls vary considerably in width, and this is largely determined by what anatomists call the zygomatic arches, the bones below the eyes on the upper jaw. In the Labrador and St Bernard these are strong and arched outwards, while in the German Shepherd dog and the Fox Terrier they are much less pronounced. Although the Labrador's head seems bigger and broader than a Fox Terrier's, this does not mean that his brain is any larger.

Some breeds, including Red Setters and Bloodhounds, have a prominent sagittal crest, the ridge on the top of the skull. Again, this does not mean that they have bigger brains, but it does allow for the attachment of extra muscles which are used for biting. It is also excellent protection from a blow on the head, and explains how some dogs may hit their heads very hard without apparent effect.

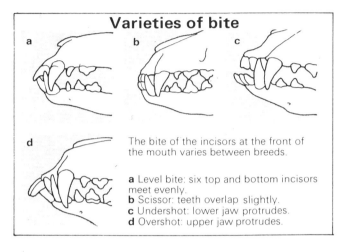

Varieties of bite

The bite of the incisors at the front of the mouth varies between breeds.

a Level bite: six top and bottom incisors meet evenly.
b Scissor: teeth overlap slightly.
c Undershot: lower jaw protrudes.
d Overshot: upper jaw protrudes.

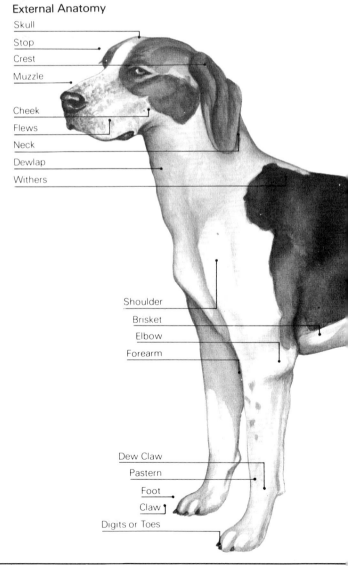

External Anatomy

Skull
Stop
Crest
Muzzle
Cheek
Flews
Neck
Dewlap
Withers
Shoulder
Brisket
Elbow
Forearm
Dew Claw
Pastern
Foot
Claw
Digits or Toes

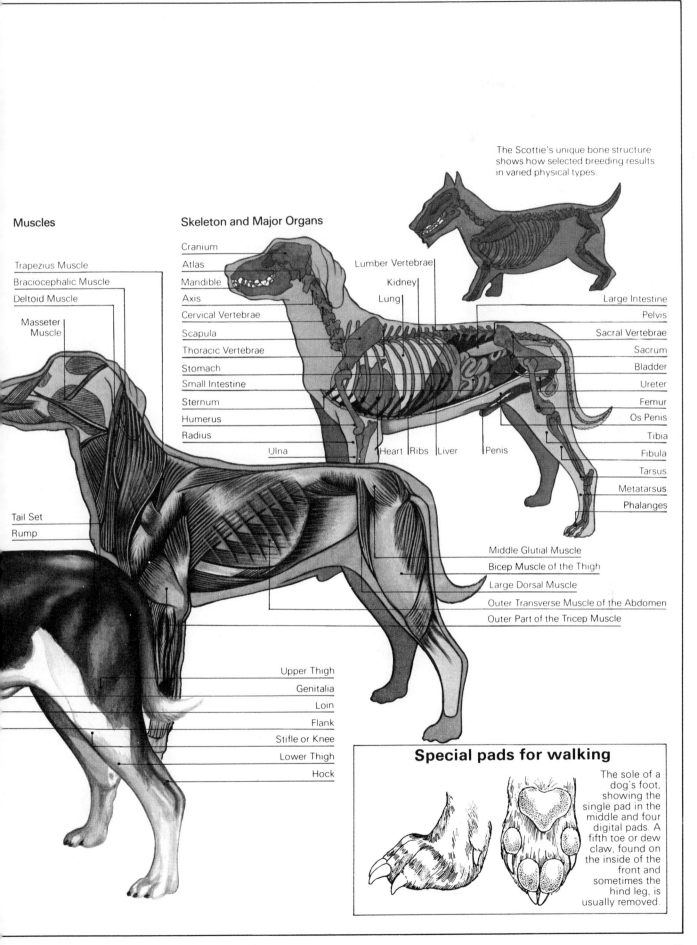

The Scottie's unique bone structure shows how selected breeding results in varied physical types.

Muscles

Trapezius Muscle
Braciocephalic Muscle
Deltoid Muscle
Masseter Muscle
Tail Set
Rump

Upper Thigh
Genitalia
Loin
Flank
Stifle or Knee
Lower Thigh
Hock

Skeleton and Major Organs

Cranium
Atlas
Mandible
Axis
Cervical Vertebrae
Scapula
Thoracic Vertebrae
Stomach
Small Intestine
Sternum
Humerus
Radius
Ulna

Lumber Vertebrae
Kidney
Lung

Heart | Ribs | Liver | Penis

Large Intestine
Pelvis
Sacral Vertebrae
Sacrum
Bladder
Ureter
Femur
Os Penis
Tibia
Fibula
Tarsus
Metatarsus
Phalanges

Middle Glutial Muscle
Bicep Muscle of the Thigh
Large Dorsal Muscle
Outer Transverse Muscle of the Abdomen
Outer Part of the Tricep Muscle

Special pads for walking

The sole of a dog's foot, showing the single pad in the middle and four digital pads. A fifth toe or dew claw, found on the inside of the front and sometimes the hind leg, is usually removed.

Hereby hangs a tail

The selective breeding of dogs has not just created a variety of skull and skeletal structures. Ears, coat types and overall colourings also vary immensely.

Presumably the original dogs had ears much like those of the wolf. These are still seen in some breeds today, especially certain types of Terrier, and are usually called fox ears. In most breeds the ears are now slightly larger, and are termed prick ears. The largest erect ears, such as those of the French Bulldog, are known as bat or tulip ears.

All the breeds with erect ears, and some with button or semi-prick ears, which curl slightly at the top, have retained the wolf's ability to move his ears backwards and forwards. This enhances the hearing, because the ears act as sound reflectors to concentrate the sound into the inner ear where it is detected.

This is not to say that dogs with hanging ears, such as the Spaniel, Pointer and Labrador, cannot hear well, but their sensitivity to sound is generally less acute than several of the other breeds. Many dogs with hanging ears have a highly developed sense of smell; the Bloodhound is an obvious example.

The early wolf-like dogs had what is known as a double smooth coat, with a thick, short underlayer and a longer outer coat which was straight and lay close and flat. Selective breeding has created all sorts of variations on this. At one extreme is the Mexican Hairless dog, which may have a few hairs on its head, though many of them have no hair at all. There are more examples at the other end of the scale: the Rough Collie has an extremely long outer coat; two Hungarian breeds, the Komondor and the Puli, have very long and dense outer coats that hang in coarse tassels; the Afghan hound has a fine but very long outer coat, which lends itself to combing.

Short coats, like those of the Weimaraner and Boxer are very common, as are wire-haired coats, where the hairs feel stiff and wavy and point in all directions. There are

Ear types

Above top The bat ears of the neat French Bulldog act as sound reflectors and contrast with the long, hanging ears of the Bloodhound. Note the latter's pendulous dewlaps.

These pictures show the extraordinary variety of dogs' coat types. **Left** The silken locks of the Afghan Hound. **Below far left to right** The strangely-marked Rhodesian Ridgeback, the Mexican Hairless Dog, and the curly coat of the Irish Water Spaniel

numerous variations on these basic types: both short and long coats can be wire-haired; long outer coats can be thin or very heavy; hair can be fluffy like a Poodle, woolly like a Husky, or frizzy like an Irish Water Spaniel.

The dog's coat, even in the short-haired breeds, acts as an extremely efficient insulator. The hair traps a layer of air between the dog's skin and the outside, protecting it against the cold. This efficient heat control means that heat loss is difficult in hot weather.

The skin of the first dogs was tight and well muscled immediately below the surface. In some breeds it has become much looser, and this is especially evident in some short-haired dogs about the face and neck. The extreme example is the Bloodhound which has what is known as a dewlap neck, layers of loose skin under its throat.

The colour and markings of the coat have also become increasingly varied through breeding. The first wolf itself showed some dark markings particularly on the face, and its colour is also highly variable across its range. This has formed the basis for all the varied markings seen in breeds of dog today, sometimes with several in one breed.

Hair of the dog

Hair of the dog
These diagrams, taken from a study made by Hildebrand in 1952, show the direction and pattern of hair growth of a dog's coat.

Running, jumping and standing still

The illustration below shows the comparative top speeds of man and various animals over a short distance. The Greyhound is one of the fastest of all dog breeds, its physique improved by selective breeding.

Man   Ostrich   Racehorse   Red Kan

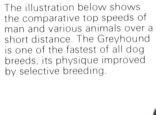

Greyhound   Jack Rabbit

mph	25		37	40	44
km	40		59	64	70

The dog's physique is essentially designed for running fast over long distances. In the Greyhound certain physical features have become exaggerated by selective breeding, creating an animal which can run over short distances at as much as 40 miles per hour.

The Greyhound has a very flexible skeleton, so that, when it is running flat out, it can bring its hind feet right forward to land well in front of where its forefeet were a moment earlier.

No other breed approaches the Greyhound's flexibility when running, and some have been bred in such a way that they can only run slowly in a somewhat cumbersome fashion. Dogs, like the Dachshund and Bassett hounds, which have long backs and short legs, land their hind feet a long way behind the imprint of the forefeet when running.

When any dog is running, its body must stay parallel with the ground. This means that a front-heavy dog, like the Bulldog, has to do much more work with his forelimbs than a dog with more even weight distribution.

The angulation of the hind limbs varies considerably from breed to breed; the modern show-type of German Shepherd dog has strongly angulated hind quarters, so that its back feet stand well behind the rear of its body.

Weight distribution, angulation and body length in relation to limb length are all likely to have important effects on the dog's balance. It is these factors which give the breeds their characteristic gaits, some of which are only apparent at certain speeds.

Dogs have a slow walk, when three feet are in contact with the ground at any one moment; this changes to a fast walk when, at times, only two feet touch the ground. When dogs trot, never more than two feet touch the ground, and these are always the diagonally opposite ones. The fastest movement is the gallop, and then only one foot touches the

Pronghorn Antelope   Cheetah

	60
	96

Top A sequence of pictures by the photographer Eadweard Muybridge, showing the body movements of a dog running. The physique is suited to long-distance running, rather than climbing, although they can be trained to do so, **right**.

ground and there may be brief moments when the dog is airborne. The only exception is the Greyhound which uses its front and back feet in pairs when galloping.

Because they were closely related to wolves, the first dogs had great stamina. This is still inherent in all breeds, but it is rarely put to the test nowadays. Even the smallest dogs, and those with large bodies and short legs, can walk great distances, but perhaps only the Husky still has to prove himself in this respect.

Huskies display immense endurance pulling sleds enormous distances in the gruelling conditions of the Arctic. One team was driven 522 miles in 80 hours. It is normal for a Husky to work eight hours a day pulling twice its own weight at between two and three miles per hour. Of all the breeds, the Husky's limb and body structure is closest to that of the wolf, and its endurance is comparable, because wolves too have been known to travel great distances in a short time. It is said that in the past the Eskimos crossed their Huskies with wolves to give them greater strength.

The dog is not so good at climbing or jumping. His feet are unable to grip surfaces and he cannot twist his legs or feet to assist his grasp. Police and military dogs can be trained to climb barriers, but they do this largely by gaining momentum, so that in effect they run up a very steep slope.

Dogs can jump over small obstacles, but they cannot make the spectacular leaps so characteristic of cats. When an animal jumps, it flexes the muscles of its hind legs very rapidly. A dog's muscles are attached to its bones in such a way that they cannot be flexed very suddenly.

Captured in full flight, this Gordon Setter shows the dog's physique to full advantage. Opportunities to exercise like this are essential for all dogs.

The dog's sense of vision

Unlike his senses of hearing and smell, a dog's vision is generally inferior to that of man. In the past many people maintained that dogs were colour-blind, but this is no longer thought to be true. In the eye there are two types of cells which can sense light, rods and cones; together they form the layer at the back of the eye known as the retina. In dogs there is a much greater proportion of rods to cones than in humans. The rods are sensitive to low levels of light, but only see in black and white. The cones are responsible for colour vision. Using very sensitive techniques, it has been shown that the few cones present in a dog's eye enable him to see colour in a rudimentary fashion. However, it is not known if he makes much practical use of this information.

The predominance of rod receptors allows the dog to see much better than humans in poor light conditions. His ability to see at night is further enhanced by the presence of a special reflective layer, known as the *tapetum*, at the back of his eye. It is the reflection from this which causes a dog's eyes to shine green or yellow-green when lit by a car's headlights at night. Any light entering the dog's eye passes through the layer of rods, and is then reflected back through them again. This increases the eye's sensitivity to light, but it also causes a loss of detail.

The dog perceives still and moving objects very differently from humans. A man can see both with ease, but a dog only seems to see objects well if they are moving, or if he himself is moving. This means that dogs see static shapes very poorly, but that they are sensitive to movement over very long distances. For example, a shepherd's hand signals can be picked up by his dog at distances of up to a mile.

Dogs are extremely sensitive to anything that makes a sudden or unusual movement, an asset made much use of by retrievers, pointers and hunting dogs. Guide dogs for the blind use this facility all the time as they lead their owners amongst crowds and across busy streets.

Another major difference between a dog's vision and that of a human is caused by the position of the eyes on the head. A man's eyes point forward and the field of view overlaps almost completely between the two eyes, whereas a dog's eyes overlap less and point to a greater or lesser extent to the side, depending on the flatness of face of the breed in question. This means that dogs judge distance less well than humans, but can detect movement over a much wider field of vision.

The diagrams below graphically illustrate the different worlds perceived by man and dog, in daylight and at night.

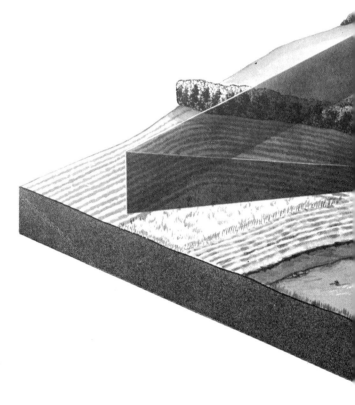

By day
The dog's sense of vision in daylight is thought to be inferior to that of man. A dog sees colour, static shapes and details very poorly, although it is very sensitive to moving objects and can see a hand waving up to a mile away.

The field of vision

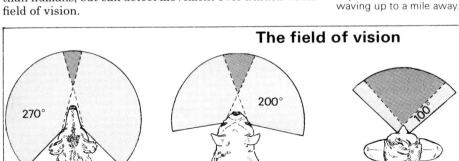

270°

200°

100°

The width of the field of vision is determined by the position of the eyes on the head. Dogs' eyes point to the side to a varying degree, depending on head shape, giving a wide view. Human eyes point forward and are able to focus more clearly.

By night
The predominance of rod
receptors in a dog's eye allows
it to see much better than
humans in poor light
conditions. Its ability to see at
night is further enhanced by a
special reflective layer at the
back of the eye, which
increases the eye's sensitivity to
light.

Ultrasonic hearing

Hearing is one of the two senses which are more highly developed in a dog than in a human; the other is of course smell. A dog's hearing is impressive in a number of ways. First of all, he can hear high notes which the human ear simply cannot detect.

Studies have shown that for low notes, the limits of detection and sensitivity are about the same for dogs and people. As frequencies rise, the dog's ear becomes progressively more sensitive than the human's, and the upper limit at which he can detect notes is much higher than that of people.

Children can detect notes up to frequencies of about 20 kiloHerz (kHz), adults rather less, while dogs are known to

A dog's sense of hearing is in some ways superior to man's.

Independently moveable. the ears act as sound shells.

Below The dog's sense of hearing is so highly developed that it can distinguish not only the sound of its owner's voice from a long way off, but the sound of particular cars and footsteps. The dog will know whether a person approaching is familiar or an intruder.

Comparative hearing of dogs and man

Comparative hearing of dog and man. Dogs are able to hear sounds that the human ear cannot detect, such as the high-pitched call of a bat.

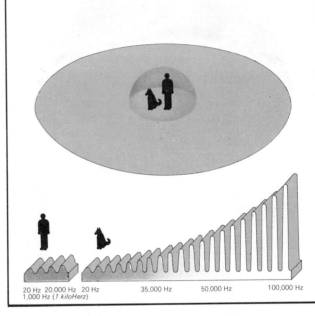

| 20 Hz 20,000 Hz
1,000 Hz (1 kiloHerz) | 20 Hz | 35,000 Hz | 50,000 Hz | 100,000 Hz |

The dog uses one ear to locate the sound source accurately.

Ears prick up to catch a maximum of sound waves.

be able to hear notes up to 35 kHz, and some authorities suggest that their limit is as high as 100 kHz.

This ultrasonic hearing – the ability to hear notes above the range of humans – enables dogs to detect the calls of many small mammals, such as shrews, mice and voles. This is obviously an evolutionary adaptation which helps the dog to hunt prey of this kind. Dogs can also hear the calls of bats, most of which are too high for human hearing.

His highly tuned ear also makes the dog responsive to the 'silent' dog whistle. As far as dogs are concerned these are no different from a normal whistle, so they can be trained to respond to them like any other sound.

Dogs are undoubtedly more sensitive to sound, ultrasonic or otherwise, than humans; they can detect most sounds from four times the distance that a human can. It is likely that they can differentiate frequencies better as well, because they can distinguish between a wide range of words used for training them.

The superiority of dogs' hearing is perhaps most commonly observed in their ability to detect the sounds of particular cars – normally their owner's – and the footsteps of particular people. Studies have been unable to show exactly how they differentiate these sounds from others, but they may be assisted in this by their ability to determine very accurately the point of origin of a sound. A dog's ears are independently moveable, and one or both can be directed towards the source of sound. In the case of footsteps, or a car, the dog can follow the route taken very accurately from sound alone.

A discerning nose

A dog's sense of smell is known to be at least 100 times better than a man's, and it has been rated more highly than this, up to 100 million times better. The true difference is probably much nearer the lower figure. The variations can be accounted for by the different methods which have been used for testing, and the variety of chemicals, with widely differing types and intensities of smell, which have formed the raw material for such tests.

Undoubtedly the dog's sense of smell is more highly developed than his other senses. All dog owners know that their pets use their noses to investigate new objects,

strange dogs and unknown people, with great interest.

The areas inside a dog's nose which detect smells are about fourteen times larger than a man's. Also, the part of a dog's brain which deals with smell is proportionally much larger and better developed than the equivalent part of a human brain. It has been estimated that there are about 40 times as many brain cells connected with smell detection in the dog as in the human. It is also conjectured that the cells in a dog's nose which detect smells may be more sensitive than those of a man, but this has not been proved.

All dogs rely on their sense of smell constantly, and some

are used by man purely to detect odours. Dogs have been used for tracking game for thousands of years, and this continues to the present day. In France dogs have been used for centuries to snuff out underground truffles.

More recently, dogs have been use by the police and the armed forces to track people and find objects and substances. A well trained tracking dog can follow the scent of a specific individual, even when this is crossed by the trails of many others; the very best trackers can follow a trail several days old. However, tracking dogs are not infallible; they can be put off the scent by adverse conditions, such as temperatures, humidity, rain, wind and competing odours.

The dog's ability to follow a track after smelling an object, or piece of clothing, belonging to a person has even been used to establish that identical twins have the same odour. A dog will follow the track of either twin after smelling an article belonging to one of them.

In the last few years, the so-called sniffer dogs have been widely used by the police and the army. These have been specially trained to smell out particular substances, especially explosives and illegal drugs, and have proved much better at finding these things than any machine.

The dog's ability to detect odours at extremely low concentrations is employed to help man in many ways.
Above an Army dog searches for hidden weapons; **left** dogs in France are trained to find truffles, elusive delicacies which only grow underground

Communication by sound

We have already discussed how sensitive the dog is to sounds. It is therefore not surprising that the dog uses this method of communication a great deal, not only for the benefit of other dogs, but with humans as well.

The communication by sound starts as soon as the puppy is born. The first sound is a yelping noise and indicates distress; this is generally caused by a painful stimulus, for example if the mother accidentally sits on the puppy. If the puppy gets cold or hungry, it makes a less intense whining or whimpering noise. The pup is presumably trying to draw his mother's attention, but studies have revealed that generally the mother will respond only if she can see the puppy as well as hear him.

Adult dogs also make a whining distress call. They do this much more frequently than adult wolves, possibly because they have been encouraged by generations of owners. Once a dog has learned that whining will elicit sympathy from his owner, he is likely to whine whenever he is distressed. It is significant that adult dogs hardly ever whine at each other.

Barking is the adult dog's most frequent sound, although some individual dogs never bark, and it is a characteristic of Basenjis, as a breed, that they bark only very rarely. Adult wolves seldom bark; when they do, it is usually to raise an alarm, issue a threat or indicate excitement during a chase.

Dogs bark in all these situations, and in others as well. That they bark so often is almost certainly due to their being encouraged to do so during their early days of domestication. A dog barking in a prehistoric settlement would arouse people to a potential threat or visitor, just as it serves this protective role in homes today. This barking on their home territory may also spread to other dogs in the neighbourhood, often with two or more dogs taking it in turns to bark. It is not clear what the barking communicates from one dog to another, except perhaps a state of alertness or excitement.

The howl is the best known call of the wolf, and this is also heard from the domestic dog, particularly from certain breeds, such as the Malamute and Siberian Husky. Analysis of howling by wolves has shown that it is a very complicated sound, and that all individuals produce a slightly different noise.

It has also been suggested that there may be more than one type of howl. One is the howl that indicates loneliness, and this is the one that another wolf or dog in earshot will take up, so that two or more are heard howling in unison. Another is the howl made by dogs on a chase – the baying hound. This may be the equivalent of the howls which wolves sometimes make after feeding, but whose communicative function is unknown.

The sound made by dogs with the most obvious meaning both to other dogs and to people is the threatening growl. When dogs fight each other, or when a frightened dog is cornered by a human, they will generally growl at their opponents, giving obvious warning.

Left The threatening growl of a frightened dog clearly conveys its intentions.
Opposite Barking may indicate alertness, a warning or defence of territory.

Communication by scent

It is hard for humans, who live in a world dominated by sight and sound, to imagine how a dog perceives his surroundings and his fellow dogs. The dog's world must be very different indeed; instead of shaking hands or looking at each other, dogs meeting will begin by checking each other's smell.

Smell is a dog's predominant sense, and it is not surprising that it is important as a major means of communication. An obvious example of this is the way that a male dog, on a walk in urban surroundings, will cock his leg to urinate on lamp posts and street corners. As well as passing urine, he leaves a little of his individual scent, produced by a special gland.

It is widely believed that male dogs leave their scent in order to mark out their territory. Male wolves and foxes behave in the same way, marking a few key places at the edges of their territory, especially those which border on the preserves of other individuals or packs.

In a town a male dog distributes his scent to a seemingly excessive degree; this is because each time he goes for a walk his odour has been covered, perhaps several times, so that he is continually having to re-establish his territory. The apparently enormous bladder of a male dog may sometimes empty, but he will nonetheless continue the attempt to mark out his territory.

Most frequently the odour of another male dog triggers urine marking, but other strong scents, such as oil or tobacco, may cause the same response. The smell of a bitch's urine when she is in oestrus is almost certain to make the male leave his own smell. At this time a bitch's urine contains a second type of pheromone, which can also be smelt coming from the bitch herself. By following the scent upwind, male dogs will quickly find her; a group of males will wait outside the house and cluster round the bitch as she is walked.

Dogs leave their scents in other ways as well. When a dog scratches the ground with his hind legs, this probably leaves an odour from the sweat glands in the toes and foot pads. Sometimes dogs seem to feel that their own scent is not sufficient, and will therefore roll in all sorts of strong-smelling substances. Wild dogs, especially dominant individuals, have been seen to do this as well. It is likely that, by making himself smell extra strong, a dog can convey to others, who meet and sniff him, that he is a top dog.

Right Two forms of communication. The people are shaking hands on meeting, while the dogs, whose predominant sense is that of smell, check each other's odour.

When a dog scratches the ground with his hind legs, he probably leaves an odour from the sweat glands in his toes and foot pads.

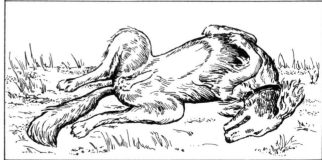

Dogs have a tendency to roll in foul-smelling substances, so that the strong smell will command respect from other dogs.

An adult male will mark out his territory by urinating on trees and lamp posts, causing other dogs to mark and claim the same areas.

The immature male adopts this position while urinating.

The female does not lift her hind leg, but squats.

Aggressive instincts

Guarding the house, defending a litter, chasing the neighbourhood cats, are all aspects of the dog's natural aggressive behaviour. A dog may also act aggressively through fear in an unknown or frightening situation, or because of intermale rivalry. Man has been able to take advantage of native canine aggressiveness, training dogs to attack on command.

Left Trained to attack only on command, this French army dog grapples with its human quarry.

The predator

If socialized towards other animals from puppyhood, like the dog and cat below, the dog will cohabit quite happily. If not, his natural instinct as a carnivore, to hunt and catch prey, will lead to the city dog's relentless pursuit of the cat, **left**.

Being a meat-eater, the dog has a strong instinct to chase and catch prey. This type of behaviour is best demonstrated by the pack of hounds chasing a fox, hare or deer, but of course, these quarry are not normally available to the domestic pet. Instead, the household dog may have to content himself with some other animal which he can chase.

Most town dogs will instinctively chase after a rabbit, if they are ever given the opportunity to do so in the countryside. Within towns cats are the only normal prey. They provide an excellent chase, without ever succumbing to any bloodshed. Usually they escape; sometimes they hide; on other occasions they end the matter with a hissing confrontation.

A pet dog visiting a farming area may chase sheep, causing a considerable nuisance, although this is unlikely if the dog has grown up with sheep. The same applies to a dog in town which has grown up with a cat in the same house. Whatever his instincts may dictate, a dog recognizes that certain other creatures share his home, and they for their part accept his presence. The development of this understanding is part of a dog's learning process – and a cat's, for that matter. For the same reason, a dog will not normally pursue or attack people unless provoked.

It may attack because it has been hurt by a human, because it is frightened, because its territory has been threatened or even because it has been trained to do so. In all of these cases, the dog is being aggressive, but he is not being predatory.

In the doghouse

BEWARE OF
THE DOG

Dogs tend to defend their territory from humans and from other dogs. If their territory is invaded by other animals, such as a horse or some other mammal, they are usually indifferent. This is probably because a dog is reared both with other dogs and with humans, so it regards each of these as its own kind and therefore a potential threat to its territory.

In a pack, the dominant dog, likely to be male and large, will take responsibility for the defence of territory. If it is alone on its own territory, even the smallest female is likely to exhibit territorial aggression, irrespective of the size or sex of the intruder. Usually, such a defence is successful by threat alone. The intruder retreats before a fight is initiated.

If a dog has been accustomed by its owners to human visitors, it is unlikely to be territorially aggressive towards these guests. This is especially true where the dog is clearly dominated by its owner. To the pet dog, the family is likely

Above and left A dog will defend its territory from other dogs and humans, regarding both as its own kind. The territory may be the dog's kennel, or that of the 'pack' – its owners' house.

to be regarded as the 'pack', and the dominant member must therefore assume responsibility for defence of territory. If the owner is seen not to show aggression towards a visitor, the subordinate dog may see no need to, either. This often leads people to think their pets are useless as guard dogs. However, in the absence of the owner, some of these dogs may behave in a quite different fashion, keenly taking the responsibility for territorial defence.

There is another, quite different, reason why a dog may be reluctant to chase a human intruder. It may simply be confused because the intruder fails to run away. If the dog's efforts consistently go unrewarded, it may gradually lose its natural territorial aggression. If, on the other hand, the visitor departs as quickly as he arrives, the territorial defence appears to have been most effective and the dog feels greatly encouraged by its success. This may explain why dogs tend to favour postmen as objects of territorial aggression.

Protective mother, aggressive male

Intermale and maternal aggression are related in that they are both influenced by levels of sex hormones produced by the testes or ovaries. Male dogs have an innate tendency to threaten or fight other males. Fighting of this kind is not practised by females, nor do males display this type of aggression towards females.

It is important to bear in mind that the different forms of aggression are not mutually exclusive; often more than one factor may be at work in inducing aggressive behaviour. For example, if two male dogs meet on what is a regular walking route for both of them, they may threaten or fight each other partly for territorial reasons and partly to vent their intermale rivalry. However, male dogs may also fight on neutral territory, such as a park or common, thereby displaying pure intermale aggression.

The dependence of this type of aggression on the male sex hormone has been demonstrated by studies of male dogs before and after castration. One study found that about half the dogs tested displayed considerably less intermale aggression after castration; fear-induced and territorial aggression were unaffected.

The dogs affected by castration were mainly those that showed definite behavioural problems, such as always threatening or attacking other male dogs when meeting them on walks. However, few male dogs display intermale aggression to a level which causes problems. This is because as puppies they are sufficiently socialized towards other dogs, and because they are trained at an early age not to show aggression. Socialization and training of this kind are very important for show dogs, because intermale or fear-induced aggression is not tolerated in the ring, and any dog displaying it will be marked down or disqualified.

Maternal aggression is seen in most species of wild animals, even in those that normally show no other type of aggression. It is thought to be dependent on the hormonal state of the female after she has given birth, as well as on the presence of her young.

While the other types of aggression are usually preceded by some type of threat, a mother may attack without warning if she fears any kind of interference with her young. However, this type of aggression has rarely been reported as causing a problem. Most people recognize that a good mother will try to protect her babies, and so leave her alone as much as possible.

Right Maternal aggression is common to most species of wild animals. As dogs generally have learned to socialize with people, the mother will happily allow a friendly person to handle her puppies, provided no threat is made to them.

This behaviour on meeting is frequently seen in wolves and dogs. The dogs face each other, tails stiffly outstretched, lips retracted.

The inferior dog will then adopt a crouching position, lowering its tail and flattening its ears.

Squatting on the ground, the submissive dog will try to lick the other's muzzle. The dominant dog stands, its ears and tail erect.

If the dominant dog continues to show aggression, the subordinate one lies on its back, urinates and shows its genital organs in total submission.

Beware of the dog

The police and the army use dogs which have been trained to attack humans. However, these animals will attack only on command; their aggression is aimed at a specific person; generally they will seize their quarry's hand, rather than making a thoroughgoing major assault on more vulnerable areas; and they will let go when their handler orders them to do so.

This complicated routine can be carried out only after extensive training. Though the end result is sophisticated, the methods of training employed follow the same principles as those used in the teaching of domestic dogs to 'sit' or 'stay'.

Statistics from hospital casualty departments have revealed that dog bites may account for as much as three per cent of total attendances. However, in only a small minority of cases – less than ten per cent – is the wound anything more than superficial. A study in New York has shown that over half of reported dog bites are incurred by people under 20. Another statistic indicated that only in a minority of cases, less than ten per cent, did a dog bite its owner or a relative of its owner. These results imply a relatively high incidence of dog bites, many of which are received by young people, usually outside the home, but the bites are almost always minor in nature.

Many of these bites are almost certainly caused by territorial aggression. A child who approaches a dog on its own territory is always at a slight risk of provoking a defensive response, which, because the child may not

recognize it as such, could end in a bite or minor attack.

However, when children or strangers are bitten, it is most likely that the dog reacts out of fear. Children are especially vulnerable in this respect. If a dog has been brought up in the sole company of adults, he may be afraid of children because they act in quite a different manner.

A child is likely to rush up to a dog with outstretched hands, possibly shouting at it, and this will appear frightening to a dog that is not used to it. If it cannot run away, or before it runs away, the dog may growl, threaten or bite the child, although in normal circumstances it shows no aggression. Couples who have no children are well advised to expose a new puppy to children as it grows up

All dogs are probably capable of fear-induced aggression,

but whether or not they express it is highly dependent on their environment and upbringing. In contrast, pain-induced aggression is more of an innate reflex, likely to be shown by any dog given a sufficiently painful stimulus. This type of aggression is rarely seen, but is occasionally encountered by veterinary surgeons giving injections, or by someone who injures a dog accidentally. It may also be provoked by someone handling a dog injured in a road accident.

The pain threshold, above which a dog will display this type of aggression, may be altered by particular circumstances. For example, when two dogs are fighting and separate, one may react aggressively to a painful blow from a human intervening, when normally it would not do so.

Above Fear-induced aggression may result from a frightening situation such as a fireworks display, so it is best to keep dogs safely indoors away from the noise.
Opposite Through careful training, the police and army can make use of, and control, the dog's aggressive instincts. The German Shepherd Dog is trained to chase and capture a suspect, seizing his arm, but releasing it on command.

Training and behaviour

Experiments by the Russian scientist Pavlov led to theories of conditioning that were to form the basis of modern training methods and theories. The poorly-trained dog may exhibit a variety of behavioural problems, ranging from destructive or aggressive tendencies, to jealousy between pet dogs and attempts to dominate its owner.

Left This well-trained dog is walking to heel at its owner's side. The dog is a Lurcher, a cross between a Terrier and a Greyhound.

The Pavlovian dog

A dog's training can progress from simple toilet training through the basic commands such as 'heel', 'sit', 'wait', 'come', 'down' and 'stay', to the complex training of dogs who compete in championship obedience classes. The essential principles used in training are similar whatever is being taught, and it is these which owners should try to understand. By the application of these principles, any dog can be taught at least the basic commands, and most much more than that.

Some breeds tend to be more responsive to advanced training than others, and it is noticeable that the majority of dogs who compete in obedience championships are border collies. When dogs fail to learn even basic training this is almost always due to the training, or lack of it, rather than the dog. Nevertheless, there is a tiny minority of dogs with genuine mental or behavioural problems due to their genetic background or severe distress early in life.

The process of training a dog is essentially that of conditioning him to perform a particular action from his normal repertoire at a specific moment. In order to train a dog successfully, it is helpful to understand how conditioning works in the dog's mind.

Two kinds of conditioning are recognized by scientists. Classical conditioning was discovered by the Russian scientist Pavlov early this century while he was working with dogs. In his now famous experiments, Pavlov found that his dogs always salivated when they smelt their food on its way. Their meal time was always signalled with a bell. Pavlov then found that after a time, his dogs would salivate in response to the bell alone, even when no food

Above The Nobel prize-winning scientist Pavlov, pictured watching an experiment of the type which led to his famous theories of animal behaviour. The sequence of drawings, **right** shows how the principle of Pavlovian conditioning is applied to two methods of house-training.

The pup will prefer to urinate on newspaper, not the floor.

The paper is moved progressively closer to the door.

The paper is finally placed outside, then dispensed with altogether.

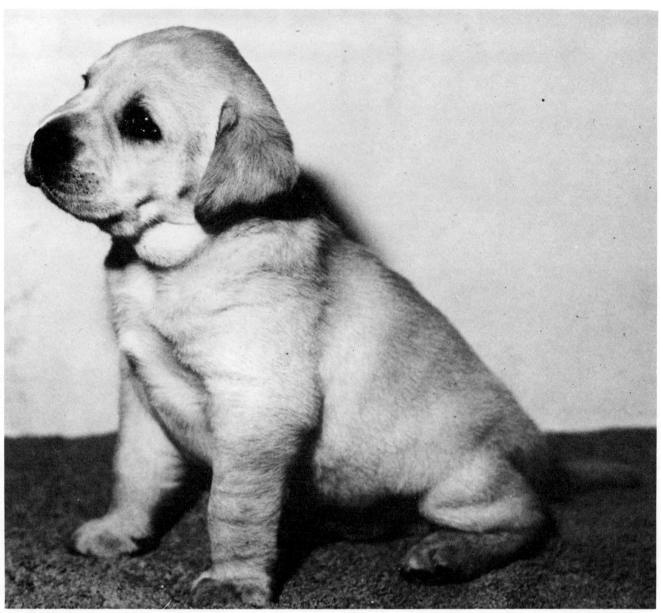

was offered. It can be seen that this type of conditioning works through a process of association in the dog's mind.

Pavlovian conditioning is useful for house training. Whenever a puppy shows signs of wanting to relieve itself, probably on awakening or after a large meal, it should be gently lifted up and taken outside. If he is taken outside sufficiently often in this way, he will very quickly come to associate the place with the act in much the same way as Pavlov's dogs made a connection between food and a bell. Puppies generally prefer to relieve themselves out of doors anyway, which facilitates this training. The same principle of conditioning can be applied to the newspaper method of house training.

After a meal, the puppy will show signs of wanting to relieve himself

He should be gently lifted up and taken outside.

Reward and punishment

The second type of conditioning is easier to understand because it is based on rewarding the dog when he has done something that pleases the owner. The principle of this type of conditioning is simply that when a dog is rewarded for behaving well, this increases the likelihood that he will behave in the same way again. As a corollary, if a dog is scolded or punished for doing something, this ought to make it less likely that he will do it on future occasions.

Most dog owners will be able to think of several occasions when these techniques have apparently been unsuccessful. A common reason for this is that a dog can get confused by what appears as a lack of consistency in the owner's behaviour. A dog can only relate a reward or reprimand to its most recent behaviour. Although a human sees that a puppy is scolded because it wet the carpet while the owner was out, it is quite unreasonable to expect the puppy to associate the two actions unless one follows immediately after the other. A delayed scolding only causes confusion in the dog's mind, because it will be behaving in a quite unrelated manner when the owner discovers the misdeed.

Although there is a place for both reward and punishment in the upbringing of a dog, as a general rule reward is always the best policy. Punishment is normally used to stop a dog doing something, or as a reprimand for a misdemeanour, but it only works if the dog is caught in the act. For example, if a dog has chewed up a pair of shoes while his owner is away and on his return the owner punishes the dog as they enter the room where the shoes are, the dog will see this as a reprimand for going into that room. The dog may then be afraid of going into the room, but he will continue to chew up shoes.

When a dog is actually caught in the act, some consideration should be given as to just how the punishment should be administered. Physical reprimand should never be too severe, and a slap on the rump or a shaking by the scruff of the neck is quite sufficient. As with reward training, it is useful to associate punishment with a verbal command such as 'bad dog', so that later on the command alone will stop the dog from behaving badly.

Punishment can have both beneficial and detrimental effects on the general behaviour of a dog. A certain amount of punishment reminds the dog that the owner is the boss, and thereby reduces the likelihood of the dog asserting himself too strongly. On the other hand, the use of too much punishment can detract from the ideal dog-to-owner relationship of loving obedience. A dog that is frequently punished can become very confused by the unpleasant treatment given him by his owner, who is also the source of what care and love he gets.

It must also be remembered that punishment may not always be received by the dog in the way it is given by the owner. To some dogs, the physical contact involved in most forms of punishment also acts as a positive stimulus. While a slap may hurt momentarily, the fact that the owner is interacting with him physically may be seen by the dog as part of a game. If a dog sees punishment as partly rewarding, its effectiveness is obviously greatly reduced.

That there are these problems associated with punishment has led some people to advocate and make electric shock collars, which administer a very small but punishing shock by remote control. While these remove the problem of the owner being directly associated with the punishment and make it easier to catch the dog in the act, they have caused a number of problems in practice. For example, if a dog is given a shock during a fight with another dog in the hope of stopping it from fighting, the dog is likely to fight more furiously than ever because of the pain it has received. Since conventional training methods are perfectly satisfactory and electric shocks are as unpleasant to dogs as they are to humans, there seem no grounds whatever for the use of these shock punishments.

A dog can only relate a reward or reprimand to its most recent activities. Punishment used to stop undesirable behaviour, such as chewing a shoe, **left**, only works if the dog is caught in the act. **Opposite** Training a dog by reward is always the best policy.

Learning obedience

Puppies vary considerably in the rate at which they mature, but informal training – especially house training – should start as soon as they are moving around independently. This is the time to teach a puppy its name and then a few basic commands. It is best to choose a short name that can be spoken clearly, will be quickly learned by the puppy, and will not be embarrassing to shout out in public.

Formal training at registered training clubs does not start until puppies are six months old, and it can be completed in about three months. However, informal training should certainly begin much earlier than this, otherwise bad habits will develop. Some of these may not become apparent until later in life, and a particularly common example is the dog that jumps up. In a small puppy this presents no problems, and indeed many owners may enjoy their puppy playing in this way. However, when dogs grow larger, it can become undesirable, irritating, or even dangerous in extreme cases, such as a St Bernard jumping up to place its paws on a small child.

It is useful to consider why a dog starts to jump up in the first place. If jumping gains the attention of the owner and results in play or affection, this is taken by the dog as a reward for the act of jumping.

A reward for a dog can take many forms. A tit-bit of food is one of the most common rewards used to encourage a good dog, or one that has just done what the owner wanted.

If food was the only possible reward, a dog would very likely overeat excessively during a formal training session. An alternative is to associate in the dog's mind a phrase such as 'good boy' by saying it each time a reward is given. 'Good boy' will then come to be considered as a reward in itself, just as the bell caused Pavlov's dogs to salivate. The other great alternative to food is affection; dogs are particularly easy to reward in this way, and this is the underlying cause of most instances of jumping up.

One of the simplest ways to eradicate an undesirable habit, such as jumping up, is simply to stop rewarding it. For example, each time a dog jumps up, the owner should walk away and ignore him. The dog should get the message fairly quickly unless the habit is too well engrained. It is also a good idea to reward the dog with affection when it behaves in the desired manner, such as standing quietly.

An alternative to ignoring the dog and hoping that undesirable or awkward behaviour will stop, is to use punishment, say a slap on the rump (not on the nose because this is very delicate). As has been seen, punishment can be useful in some circumstances, but with a jumping dog, it is unlikely to help. This is because the dog may well be totally confused by a change from the previous reward for this behaviour to sudden punishment for doing what to the dog is the same thing. Looked at from the dog's point of view this is illogical and disturbing and may therefore lead to other behaviour problems.

Puppies should not be allowed to develop the habit of jumping up, as this behaviour is undesirable in a fully-grown dog, **below. Left** A tit-bit of food or a show of affection are the most common rewards used to encourage a good dog during training.

The well-trained dog

The commands that are generally taught as basic training are 'heel', 'sit', 'wait', 'come', 'down' and 'stay'. Although the formal lessons at training schools do not start until a puppy is six months old, it should be possible to go some way towards teaching these commands before that time. With a young puppy, and also even with an older dog, it is important to give training in a large number of short lessons rather than marathon sessions during which the dog will quickly get tired. The sessions should be made enjoyable, with plenty of attention for the dog both during it and afterwards.

The way the basic commands are taught is based upon the methods of conditioning, reward and punishment already described. There is no fixed order in which the commands should be learnt, but the dog is often trained to walk to heel before anything else. The dog should walk steadily at the pace of the owner, close to his or her leg, but not in front of it; it is customary for the dog to be taught to walk on the left hand side.

Normally the puppy or dog will try to rush off ahead from time to time, particularly when he smells something or sees another dog. When this happens, the dog should be checked with a sharp jerk on the lead, and at the same time the command 'heel' should be given. The dog should learn that it is more comfortable to walk in the correct way, and it will also associate the command with the action. If the dog is well trained to walk to this command, it should continue to do so even when it is off the lead; this should first be attempted in a quiet open space.

Be careful putting on the lead, so as not to frighten the pup.

The dog may be playful or nervous during the first lessons.

Hold the lead in the right hand, reassure or admonish with the left.

The lead should be slack, with the pup walking at the owner's pace.

Push the dog's hindquarters down, to reinforce the command to sit.

Teaching the dog to sit against a wall may help the learning process.

The command 'sit' is often taught next. This can be done in more than one way, with or without the use of a food reward. Usually the hindquarters of the dog are pushed down into the sit position at the same time as the command 'sit' is given. The dog then learns the command by associating the word with the act, especially if the word is also spoken when the dog moves into the sit position of its own accord.

However, as an alternative it can be a good idea to teach the command entirely or in part by using a food reward. It is well worthwhile teaching a family dog to sit quietly when he is about to be fed, instead of pestering the person preparing his meal, or worse still a group of people sitting around a dinner table.

To teach 'sit' in this way, use a small food reward and give it to the dog so that it takes it gently, but only as soon as it has gone into a sitting position. The word 'sit' should be spoken at the same time. The dog is more likely to sit automatically if it is backing away from you up against a wall, so this situation can be engineered to help the process along. If this technique is used repeatedly, the dog will come to associate the sitting both with being fed and the command 'sit'. It is a relatively simple next step to get the dog to sit quietly while its food is being prepared. The meal itself will then further reward the act of sitting.

The dog that pesters people for tit-bits at a dinner table may be amusing at times, but this is an undesirable habit, and should never be allowed to start. It usually begins with a waste scrap from the side of a plate which the dog immediately accepts. The problem is that the dog quickly comes to expect a scrap at every meal, and only quietens down when he gets it; he has now trained the owner. If the dog is trained to sit or lie down during meals, and is never rewarded with scraps, the habit will never begin.

The basic commands should be taught in a series of short lessons rather than marathon sessions, and these should be made enjoyable, with plenty of attention for the dog.
Left Walking to heel is one of the first things a dog learns – not to rush ahead, but to walk with the owner even when off the lead.

His master's voice

The traditional way to train a dog to stay is to start by doing repeated exercises with the dog on the lead. The lead must be long, or else extended by attaching a cord, to allow for an increasing distance between the dog and owner. The dog is put in a sitting position and the owner then moves slowly away, repeating the word 'stay'. Some people also find it useful to use a hand signal to reinforce the verbal command.

At first the owner should only back up a short distance and then return and praise the dog if he has not moved. If the dog moves, the owner should say 'bad dog' and put him back in his original position. The distance between the owner and the dog should then be slowly increased so that the dog continues to stay still on the majority of occasions. When the dog responds successfully to the stay command the owner should return, rather than allow the dog to come towards him thinking all is over, because this will prevent the learning process.

Once the dog will stay while the owner moves several yards away, it is time to move on and teach the dog to come when called. The lesson should again begin with the dog on a long lead. The dog should be told to stay and when the owner is some distance away, he should tug gently on the lead and say 'come' at the same time. The dog should learn this command quickly because he will be much happier to come up to the owner and be petted rather than be left sitting alone. However, this command is a very important one for the dog to learn well, since it is essential for the owner to be able to call a dog to him in certain circumstances, such as when the dog is loose with other dogs in a park, or is about to rush away across a road. Once a dog has been trained in this way on the lead, he should be given training off the lead.

A whole range of other commands can be taught using similar methods to those already described, all of which depend on the conditioning techniques of rewarding a dog with food or affection, or repeatedly associating a command with a particular act.

The most useful commands to teach next are 'down' and 'fetch'. 'Down' can be taught in a similar way to 'sit', with the frontquarters of the dog being pushed if necessary. Most dogs will fetch readily and therefore little teaching may be required, but a problem can arise if the dog fails to let go of the object. For this reason, an occasional food reward may help because the dog will have to release the object to get the food. The reward can be given first when the dog is holding an object, say a stick, in its mouth. He will then start to come with the stick hoping for a reward. The reward can then be given less often, and the word 'fetch' used each time the dog goes to pick up an object, perhaps one that has been thrown.

It is important that dogs learn to eliminate on command; they can be taught this quite successfully so that they can be given the instruction only when they are in a suitable place. The method used for teaching is similar to other training with a command such as 'clean boy' being given each time the puppy performs. It will soon associate the two. That this method can be successful has been demonstrated by the British guide dogs for the blind, all of which are taught in this way.

Left Using methods which depend on various conditioning techniques, the owner trains the dog to obey basic commands. It should be given lessons without the lead, once it has learned to come and stay.

The lesson begins with the dog sitting at the end of a long lead.

The owner moves slowly away, repeating the word 'stay', perhaps using a hand signal to reinforce the command.

Once the dog has learned to stay, it is taught to come when called. The owner should tug gently on the lead and say 'come' at the same time.

Frequent rewards of affection and tit-bits of food are often given.

The leader of the pack

Below The dominated owner will have great problems with the dog, being unable to control it on walks and victimized by it in the house. He or she must retrain it, gradually, to be dependent and obey orders.

Dogs can develop what appear to be psychological problems, although in reality, these are social problems. A common behaviour problem arises from the dog's instincts as a pack animal. In the pack, the dog expects the presence of a leader. It may consider itself to be an ideal candidate for the leadership, and attempt to establish itself in this position. Usually, it will regard its owner as the pack leader, but in some instances it may try and achieve for itself the position of dominance. This problem is more common with the larger breeds.

If a dog dominates the family, it can cause all sorts of difficulties. It will refuse to obey orders, be uncontrollable on walks, 'defend' its owner against visitors and aggressively reserve its right to occupy the best armchair. In some cases, the dog may seek to dominate the whole family; in other instances, it may simply decide that one particular member of the household deserves a lower position than itself in the social structure. Either way, these problems can be solved only with difficulty.

The best time to correct the dog's behaviour is when it first tries to assert its dominance, probably when it is quite a young puppy. Holding it down by the scruff of the neck if it ever becomes assertive should be effective.

If the problem already exists in an adult dog, or starts to appear, such treatment may not be successful. However, in all but the worst cases, the application of suitable psychology should be of some help.

However dominant the dog may be, it must still look to its owner for food. It will also still enjoy a little play and affection from time to time. The owner can therefore use food and affection as a reward in the re-training of the dog. The dog must be taught by conditioning that these can only be obtained from the person whom it has previously tried to dominate, and to associate this with good behaviour.

To succeed, the technique must be used slowly and gradually, and the dog must not be provoked to aggression. The person, or people, who are most dominated by the dog should take complete care of it. In particular, they should handle all those activities which give pleasure to the dog. When the dog indicates an inclination to obey, they should use the food reward in an effort to engage it in basic training: to sit or stay, for example. Other family members should ignore the dog except on unpleasant occasions such as a visit to the vet.

Menacing facial expression of the dominant dog.

Submissive pose of a dog which accepts its owner as pack leader.

Dogs on the loose

Male dogs may cause their owners more problems than female dogs. There are three reasons for this. First, male dogs are more likely to try to assert dominance, with all the resulting difficulties. Secondly, male dogs tend to be motivated more strongly sexually, and this can lead to a range of problems in that area. Thirdly, there are several behaviour traits, seen in male dogs, which are almost never displayed by bitches.

The first of these is roaming, or straying. It is quite common for some male dogs to disappear for hours, days or even weeks, and then return home. Sometimes they may be in good condition suggesting they have been looked after; other times they may be extremely dishevelled. It is not known why dogs should roam in this way, although interestingly male cats have this very same tendency. It is only possible to speculate that the males of both species may at times be affected by an instinctive urge to in-vestigate a wider area than their normal home range. It is known that males of species closely related to the dog, such as the fox, often have a range of several square miles, which makes the range of most dogs very small.

A male dog may also stray when he detects a bitch on heat and he may then try to stay near her during the duration. Roaming is not only confined almost entirely to males in both dogs and cats, but it also seems to be directly linked to the male sex hormone. A study by Drs. Hopkins, Schubert and Hart of the University of California showed that, following castration, almost 95 per cent of habitual roamers lost the habit, either rapidly or gradually.

The same study also investigated a second behaviour problem confined almost entirely to male dogs, that of urine marking in the home. This is, of course, normal outside the house, but dogs are trained as puppies not to do it indoors. Nevertheless, its function is essentially that of

territorial marking, and the tendency to mark indoors sometimes reappears in adult male dogs, which were previously housetrained as puppies. This may be one of the many indications of a dog that is dominant within the household, the urine marking being used to establish its territory beyond dispute.

The treatment for this can be the same as that already recommended for the dominant dog. An alternative is castration, or possibly a hormonal treatment that can be obtained from a veterinary surgeon.

Dogs of this kind have not gone wild, but they do behave as packs in many distinct and observable ways. For example, it is frequently obvious that a dominance hierarchy exists. If the pack moves from one area to another, it is very often the same dog that leads the way.

Packs such as these are very much temporary since they only exist for short periods each day. Also they tend to have a different membership from day to day. Partly because of this, they are likely to interact with each other in a range of different ways, since they cannot achieve the high level of understanding between individuals that seems to exist in a wolf pack, or indeed in a pack of the second type of stray dogs – the feral dogs.

Feral dogs differ from free-ranging dogs in that they have no permanent homes, and support themselves quite independently from humans, except on odd occasions when they may be left some scraps. Within the developed world the feral dog is at present found only in parts of the United States, at least in any noticeable numbers. They represent a problem in some areas, and therefore some detailed studies of them have been made.

Feral dogs are generally distinguished by being in very poor condition, often emaciated; they do not allow humans to come near, and they become aggressive if cornered. Interestingly they often live as individuals, rather than in packs. The packs that do exist are usually small, made up of only two or three dogs. This is probably due not so much to their behaving inherently differently from other dogs, but more to the pressure of the environment in which they live. They usually find it difficult to obtain adequate food, and if they lived in groups this would obviously be an even greater problem. In the United States, they are often threatened by dog catching agencies, which are more likely to chase a group of dogs than an individual.

Studies have shown that feral dogs rarely manage to rear their own puppies. This means that their continuing existence is dependent on recruitment from tame and free-ranging dogs, and is therefore, in effect, entirely in the hands of the dog-owning public.

Left Male dogs can cause their owners problems by a tendency to stray. They may roam for short or long periods, sometimes forming into packs.
Above The feral dog lives as a scavenger, raiding rubbish bins in city areas in search of food.

The canine vandal

Whatever training it is given, every dog retains its own personality. This is dependent on many factors, the genetic background of the dog, its early socialization with people, the way the owner interacts with it, and its early training.

Behaviour which causes problems for the owner can arise from any one of these factors, and for a few other reasons as well. One of the commonest difficulties is destructive behaviour. This can take many forms, including scratching at doors or furniture, or knocking over valuable items, but the most common is the chewing of clothes, shoes, carpets or furniture while the owner is out.

It is best to begin a definite programme when the dog is first acquired; the dog should be left in one room while the owner stays quietly in another for increasing lengths of time. If the dog is quiet for a few minutes, the owner should go back in and praise this good performance. If the dog is heard to make destructive noises, the owner should either leave it until it is quiet and then reward it with praise, or else give some sort of punishment. Probably the best sort of punishment is a scolding through the door. If the owner goes and punishes the dog physically, the pleasure of the owner's company may outweigh the pain of the slap, thereby actually encouraging the dog to be destructive.

If an early training of this kind is not undertaken, there is an ever-present danger of the dog either destroying something, or barking persistently while the owner is out. These activities are similar since both probably arise through boredom when the dog is left on its own. It is very easy for the owner to encourage accidentally, or reinforce, this type of behaviour when he returns; even if he scolds his pet, the dog will associate this with his behaviour immediately preceding the scolding. More than likely, the dog will have heard his owner returning and will therefore have stopped barking or chewing the carpet some time before his owner reaches him. It is therefore possible for destructive behaviour or barking to become conditioned accidentally, making the habit doubly difficult to break.

Bad habits of this type are best removed by trying to condition the dog to good behaviour instead. One approach is to give the dog a ball, ring or some other toy to chew when he is alone. If dog and owner play games with this toy, the dog will develop an attachment to it, and can be given it each time the owner goes out. A training programme can then begin starting with short departures and slowly lengthening the time. The departures should be made as realistic as possible, with all the usual noises and actions associated with leaving the house. If the dog has chewed the wrong thing, or if it has barked persistently, it should be ignored by the 'returning' owner so that this behavoiur is discouraged. As the programme continues, hopefully the dog will come to associate quiet, good behaviour while alone with a happy, playful reunion with its owner.

Left When left alone in the house or car, the pup should be provided with its own toys, such as the leather bone in this picture, to avoid destructive behaviour which may damage furniture or clothes.

Aggressive behaviour

It is quite natural for dogs to exhibit many forms of aggression, and these have already been described. Displays of aggression which pose problems for owners thus have many different causes and several potential cures.

The dog which bites the mailman is giving vent to his territorial aggression, but it is, of course, the same type of aggression which makes him attack a burglar. It is almost impossible to train a dog to differentiate between such intruders, and it is therefore extremely difficult to stop a dog threatening a postman. It is best for responsible owners to prevent the dog making unwanted territorial attacks, by keeping it indoors at times of routine visits by the mailman.

Territorial aggression may also be practised on visiting friends or relations, but this is less common because the presence of the owner ought to inhibit the dog's feeling of aggression. However, if the dog dominates the owner in the manner already outlined, its territorial aggression may well be more freely exhibited. If this is the case, the dominance problems should be treated in the way described elsewhere, because this is the underlying cause of the aggressive behaviour.

If the aggression is entirely territorial in nature, a different type of training is required. Physical punishment is never a good solution for aggression, so a less severe punishment should be given, for example putting the dog alone in a room for a short period. This should be done each time the dog barks or growls at visitors.

Aggression caused by fear is also very common, and the relatively high incidence of minor dog bites is probably due to fear of strangers, along with some territorial component. Aggression of this kind is revealed in the dog's facial expression and body posture, as has been described. It can be cured by a programme of socializing the dog more fully with a wide range of people, including the type that the dog particularly tends to threaten.

The best technique is a process called desensitization: gradually introducing the dog to the source of fear in small steps of increasing intensity. The dog should first be approached by someone it knows, and fears; the person should keep his distance at first so as to minimize the likelihood of frightening the dog. The dog should be rewarded with affection, praise or food if he shows no fear. On no account should the dog be rewarded if he responds with any measure of aggression. The person should come gradually closer to the dog on successive occasions, but this should not be attempted too quickly because the learning will then be less strong. Once the dog responds satisfactorily to someone he knows, the same process can be undertaken with a stranger. The whole sequence should be repeated, and then perhaps once again with the type of person that previously provoked most aggression, say an adult man or a playful child.

Cures of this kind are slow and never certain, but they are most likely to succeed if they are undertaken without delay when the dog first exhibits anti-social aggression.

Right This dog is exhibiting the most common form of aggression, that caused by fear, in a dangerous situation.

Sexual problems

Some of the most common and persistent problems for dog owners arise from their dog's sexuality. These difficulties range from the dog who appears completely uninterested in other dogswhen the owner wants it to breed, to the dog who frequently attempts to mount the legs of people instead of other dogs when the owner wants it to breed, to the dog who frequently attempts to mount the legs of people instead of dogs and with people in much the same way. It is therefore not really surprising that dogs sometimes get confused as to whether they are dogs or people when it comes to reproductive behaviour.

Most of a puppy's socialization occurs when he is between five and fourteen weeks old. During this period, dogs learn their social response towards dogs, humans and any other animals with which they have contact. It is also likely that the dog develops its future sexual preferences during this period.

Therefore a dog which is removed from its parents at a very early age, say about five weeks, and is then brought up only with people, may become so strongly socialized towards people that it believes these, rather than other dogs, are its potential sexual partners. This belief can reveal itself in more than one way. It is quite common for dogs, male or female, to refuse to mate with other dogs. Sometimes the dog is put off by what it regards as an unpleasant experience, but frequently such dogs do not appear even to recognize other dogs as potential partners.

A more awkward problem is the dog or bitch which

displays apparently aberrant sexual behaviour towards people. A dog which tries to mount a person's leg can cause great embarrassment. Mounting of this kind is sometimes practised by bitches as well; this may seem unnatural, but it is almost certainly a frustrated response on behalf of a bitch who is not sufficiently socialized towards her own species to accept advances from a male dog.

This sort of behaviour tends to be persistent, even in the face of disappointment, and difficult to cure because it comes naturally to the dog, who therefore may not readily respond to punishment. Even when attempts are made to avoid situations where the dog can behave in this way, the tendency is not extinguished, but lies latent until the right stimulus presents itself.

These factors make sexual problems more difficult than most others, but conditioning may sometimes succeed. An alternative is to consult a veterinary surgeon who may be able to help in one of two ways: either by castrating a male, after which sexual behaviour will decline rapidly; or by prescribing a hormone preparation, although this may be a temporary rather than a permanent solution.

The option with the best long-term chance of success may well be to try and help by bringing the dog into contact with others of its own species. Most sexual problems occur with single pet dogs; greatly increased contact with other dogs may help to heighten a dog's – even an older dog's – awareness of his own species, and so may cure or alleviate the problem.

Unlike the puppies, **left**, and the dogs, **above**, single pet dogs may develop sexual problems, regarding the humans they live with as potential sexual partners.

Dog in a manger

When two pet dogs have been brought up together from puppyhood, they generally get on together extremely well. Problems are more likely to arise when a dog is brought into a house with another dog already in residence. More often than not, no conflict will occur; when it does, it will generally be resolved without too much difficulty.

When there are two or more pet dogs in the home, they will always develop a dominance relationship among themselves, which may or may not be readily apparent to the owner. If there is a stable dominance relationship, the two or more dogs will all live peaceably together. However, any change in this relationship will almost always result in conflict between the dogs. Sometimes the owner will not even notice this, because it will all be over very quickly,

perhaps in one brief encounter. At other times there may be a long power struggle with frequent fighting.

A change in dominance relationship can occur for many reasons. Where there is an older dog already in residence and a new puppy of a larger breed is brought in, a problem will very likely arise when the younger dog grows up, because at some stage it will almost certainly try to take over the top position. This is likely to be resisted by the previous top dog, and there can be a prolonged canine equivalent to a power struggle, with frequent fighting, growling, or competition over food and prized objects.

A change in dominance can also be brought about if the top dog suffers a minor illness or injury; this may not be sensed by the owner, but will be noticed by the underdog.

The owner may be unaware of the established pack order between pet dogs, favouring the underdog – the smaller, older or weaker.

This will upset the natural order, causing the dominant dog to defend its position by attacking the favourite.

The owner should show affection to the dominant dog. The position of both dogs will be defined, the hierarchy accepted.

A natural dominance relationship between two dogs can be easily upset by the attitude of the owner. The owner will often favour the older dog rather than the newcomer, or the smaller than the larger, thereby taking the familiar stance of favouring the underdog.

Unfortunately, dogs do not view things in this way because, in their hierarchy, the upper dog should have precedence over the lower one and more attention from the individual ranking above it, namely the owner. If the owner favours the underdog when the top dog is present, the latter will view this as 'insubordination' on the part of the underdog, and may well threaten, or even attack, him in the owner's presence. This leads many owners to protect the underdog or scold the dominant dog, but this in fact does not have the result the owner intends. The dominant dog will feel compelled to attack the other dog to maintain its dominance, even when the owner is there and the other dog knows it is being protected.

It is indeed difficult for owners, but in these circumstances they should try to reassure, and show affection for, the dominant dog rather than the underdog. This is, in fact, best for both dogs because otherwise the fighting may continue almost indefinitely. Also, by emphasizing the dominance hierarchy of owner, dominant dog and underdog, a situation is established which all, especially the dogs, can readily accept. Even the underdog will be happier to know exactly what it can, or cannot, do, instead of having to rely on the protection of the owner.

Fighting between pet dogs may occur when the established dominance relationship changes through illness, or the younger dog grows assert itself. There may be a power struggle with fighting over food, **left**, or prized toys. The owner must handle the situation carefully.

Dogs trained for special work

Early man first used dogs for hunting. Today they work for man in a great variety of roles, as gun dogs, herding dogs and for mountain rescue. Inherent tendencies, such as the instinct to retrieve or natural aggressiveness, combined with the capacity to learn, have enabled man to train dogs for difficult military and police work, for entertainment and for use in certain sports.

Left This Border Collie keeps the sheep from moving by the force of its look, known as 'giving sheep the eye'.

Hounds and hunters

Right The role of hunting dogs is mainly sporting today, but formerly they were needed for survival, as in the Dürer etching, **above**. **Below right** The Persian Saluki was used to course gazelles. **Opposite bottom** Wire-haired Fox Terriers were bred to pursue the fox underground.

Many of the first tame dogs were used for herding and guarding animals, but dogs were used for hunting at an equally early stage, and are still bred for this role after several thousand years. The first hunting dogs were probably very fast runners and would have been used to chase various types of quarry. Their descendants include several different breeds which are generally grouped together as hounds.

Many hounds are named directly after the quarry they have been bred to chase, for example the Foxhound, Deerhound, Otterhound and Irish Wolfhound. Other famous hunting breeds include the Russian Borzoi which was used to hunt wolves, the Greyhound which chased many types of game – hares, jackals and gazelles for example – and the Beagle which was bred to hunt hares.

Nowadays almost all hunting dogs are kept for sport rather than survival, and they frequently hunt in packs; English Foxhounds and Beagles are almost always used in

this way, the hunters following on horseback or foot.

Chasing is not the only way that dogs can catch game, and the existence of several specific breeds – some of them hounds – reflects this. Dachshund in English means badger hound, and these were bred small so that they could go down into badger sets, confront the badger and either drive it out or hold it still. The Dachshund's bark would tell the owner where the badger was, so that it could be dug out. Dachshund owners may have noticed that their dogs are very good at digging.

The Terriers were originally bred for a similar purpose in England, and comprise a group of dogs separate from the hounds. There are now several breeds, and some of the larger ones are used for hunting above ground, especially in thick undergrowth. Some terriers were bred to catch very small vermin: rats, stoats, weasels and so on. The Manchester Terrier, formerly called the Black and Tan Terrier, was originally bred for this purpose.

On the scent

While some dogs have been bred and trained to catch and kill prey, others have been developed to assist with hunting, rather than to do the killing themselves. Their origins can be traced back about 2500 years to a report by the Greek historian, Xenophon. He described dogs that, instead of chasing prey on sight, would stand completely still, looking at the animal or bird, quivering with excitement. This trait was originally exploited by falconers.

The breeding of dogs of this kind was stimulated considerably by the invention of the gun. Mainly using their sense of smell, the dog, or dogs, would search out the game, and indicate its position by standing still and pointing its head in the appropriate direction. On command the dog would then move forward to flush and retrieve the prey.

Special training is required for dogs to carry out these functions well, because they tend naturally to chase the game rather than stop and point at it. Another vital requirement is that the dogs are not gun-shy. Training is given by subjecting young dogs to loud noises at close range, and praising them when they show no fear.

In the United States and England there is a tendency to use one dog for searching, indicating the prey and flushing, and another for retrieving. The various breeds of Pointer, Setter and Spaniel are used for the first three stages, the many types of Retriever are all specialists in the last phase.

On the continent of Europe, sportsmen have tried to develop more versatile dogs which can assist their owners in all aspects of their shooting. This has an obvious advantage, but it can lead to an overall lower quality of performance. The Münsterländer and Weimaraner are both multi-purpose gundogs of this kind.

A well-trained Labrador Retriever waits for permission to move.

Spaniels explore every bit of undergrowth to locate the prey.

Two pointers, having picked up the scent, freeze in the classical pose: nose held high, foreleg lifted, tail an extension of the bodyline.

Opposite page, top left one of the oldest breeds, the Springer Spaniel, was used to 'spring' game, as shown in this early etching. **Centre** two Weimaraners – a special breed of gundog developed at the court of Weimar to work as both pointer and retriever. **Below** a pheasant shoot.

The good gundog should return swiftly, with the prey held very gently in its mouth; the game when released, should be unmarked

Some dogs were specially bred to retrieve the prey from water.

The obedient gundog should relinquish the bird immediately

Dogs for sport and entertainment

It was quite natural that, as hunting with dogs ceased to be essential and became a sport, so dogs came to be used in other sports which had nothing to do with hunting at all. The most popular of these nowadays is greyhound racing where the dogs chase a simulated 'hare' around a roughly circular track. This is practised in many countries, attracting a great number of spectators and large sums of money in bets. Other breeds of dog, notably whippets, are raced in a similar way. For other types of racing, such as hare coursing, live prey are used, but this is on the decline and has been made illegal in many countries.

In the past, dogs were used in many sports which are now considered cruel and are no longer permitted. One of these was bull-baiting, which in England started at least 700 years ago. It was a popular sport and dogs were bred especially for it, giving rise to the Bulldog, and later the Bull Terrier and Staffordshire Bull Terrier.

Bull-baiting took place in special pits and the dogs sometimes fought other animals or dogs instead of bulls. This was banned in England in 1835, and in other countries at around the same time. However, it continued illegally for some years, and other sports, such as rat catching for

Canine capers in the big top

The world of circus and side-show entertainment makes full use of the dog's ability to learn quite complex tricks, such as leaping through flaming hoops and turning somersaults. **Below** A typical act with a troupe of Poodles trained to walk on their hind legs. The bottom picture shows 'Johnny Watson's Canine Wonders – a Howling Success'.

Dogs have long been used in popular sports which attract huge crowds and large sums of betting money.
Below Greyhound racing flourishes in many countries today. **Right** The dog's ability to hunt rats was exploited in the now illegal sport of ratting.

which the Manchester Terrier in particular was used, were introduced. Heavy gambling was involved, and some remarkable feats were recorded, such as one Manchester terrier which killed 100 rats in 6 minutes and 32 seconds.

Sport of this kind has now almost completely disappeared, but dogs still have a considerable entertainment role. Sheepdog trials consistently attract large audiences, as do displays by police and army dogs who exhibit such skills as climbing fences and jumping through flaming hoops. In circuses specially trained dogs perform such feats as walking on two legs and turning somersaults.

Trained to find prey for the hunter, Pointers will stop still in this typical pose, indicating its position and awaiting further instructions.

Herding dogs

One of the first uses to which man put the dog was the herding, driving and protecting of sheep, cattle and deer. There are many regional dog breeds across the world, whose names reflect their former, and in some cases current, function: the Pyrenean Sheepdog, the Belgian cattle dog, the German Shepherd dog, the Yugoslavian Sheepdog and the old English Sheepdog.

The exact use for which these dogs were bred varied greatly from place to place. The Pyrenean Sheepdog originally guarded herds of domestic animals from wolves and bears in remote mountain regions. Another large breed, the old English Sheepdog probably had a similar function originally, but was later used for herding sheep and for driving cattle.

The supreme sheepdog today is the Border Collie, the border being that between England and Scotland. It is these that compete in sheepdog trials, where they have to demonstrate their skill under the orders of a farmer or shepherd. Like many breeds of sheepdog, Border Collies have a natural herding instinct which can be seen even when they are not specially trained. A special characteristic is known as the 'eye', the ability to hold a sheep, or group of sheep, still just by staring directly at them. This is an excellent example of the behaviour of a dog, as well as its appearance, becoming a breed characteristic after generations of selection.

A new breed of sheepdog known as the Kelpie has been developed in Australia. An unusual characteristic of these is that they will run over the backs of tightly herded sheep; appropriately this has become known as 'backing'. The

Specially bred for herding

Above top A Kelpie rests on the backs of yarded sheep. These dogs, prized for their toughness and intelligence, were bred from Scottish Collies for the rough terrain, hot summers and bleak winters of Australia's grazing lands, and have now been exported to several other countries, including the USA and Kenya.

Above 'Giving the sheep the eye. The well-trained dog, anticipating every move, will not bark or bite, but will round up the sheep with infinite patience, working tirelessly and quickly.

Australians have also bred a new type of dog for herding cattle. This is known as the 'heeler' because it nips at the cattle's heels to drive them along.

Different behaviour characteristics are necessary in dogs which are to drive cattle. They do not even need to be very large; Welsh Corgis can drive cattle very effectively, and records of their use date back to 1000 years ago.

While the herding and driving breeds of sheep and cattle dog often have short coats, it is noticeable that many of the breeds developed for guarding animals have exceptionally long coats to protect them against the cold. The Old English Sheepdog and the Pyrenean Mountain dog are good examples, but the most remarkable coats belong to two Hungarian breeds of guard dog, the Puli and the Komondor. Their coats hang in long woolly tassels.

Above left Picture showing three generations of Pyrenean Mountain Dog, bred to guard flocks in all kinds of weather in steep mountain regions.
Above and left Guarding and herding dogs work together in perfect understanding with their owners.

Seeing Eyes

Guide dogs for the blind, or 'seeing eyes' as they are called in the United States, must rank as the most valuable group of trained dogs. The selection of these dogs is extremely important, because although all dogs can be taught basic training, comparatively few can be trained satisfactorily as guide dogs. Only the larger breeds are suitable, and among these, the German Shepherd dog is most popular in the United States, and the Labrador Retriever in Britain, where there is a planned breeding programme to provide most of the new puppies. As a result of this programme the percentage of puppies that are successfully trained has risen steadily, showing the effectiveness of selective breeding.

The puppies selected for training are bitches, mainly

Difficult tasks prepare the dog for future, responsible work.

He must never cross when traffic is moving.

He must avoid low objects and dangerous overhangs.

Guide dogs must learn to negotiate escalators.

because they are less dominant and less easily distracted by other dogs. They are spayed to avoid the problems of their coming into heat.

A potential guide dog's training begins when she is boarded out with a volunteer puppy walker at the age of about two months. The puppy walker will look after her until she is between 10 and 12 months old, and will give the basic house and obedience training. The puppy will also be familiarized with traffic, stores, railroad stations, bridges, buses and other dogs, and will be taught to walk in the way that will be necessary in the future. This is in the centre of the pavement, on the left hand side and slightly in front of the owner. The puppy will be taught to sit in a special way, bringing her legs up to her front legs, because this is more convenient for her future partner.

After these months with the puppy walker, the potential guide dog goes to a training centre for assessment. Certain faults, such as cat chasing, oversensitivity to loud noises, or a generally unsound temperament, will exclude a dog unless they are quickly corrected. If the dog is not rejected, training in guide dog harness begins.

In the final stage of training, the dog establishes its relationship with its new blind owner. The owners have to be shown how to handle their dogs without upsetting the earlier training, and have to learn to rely on the dog for their mobility. The owner also has to gain respect from the dog so he can control it effectively.

The dog is only a guide dog when it is in the harness. At other times, it loves affection and behaves like any other dog. It is only when the dog is working that its superb degree of training is evident.

Above and left In harness, the superbly-trained guide dog becomes the 'eyes' of his owner. At other times, he is a normal, playful dog, needing affection.

In the service of man

THE NEWFOUNDLAND DOG.

As well as hunting and herding, dogs have performed many other working roles for thousands of years. In snowbound areas dogs were, and still are to a lesser degree, important beasts of burden. Although dogs are much smaller than most animals used for pulling carts and sledges and consequently can pull lesser weights, their endurance of the cold and ice makes them highly suitable for such conditions. The Huskies and similar breeds of the north are best known in this connection, but Swiss Mountain Dogs also have a long history as pack animals in the alpine region.

The dog's qualities of endurance together with his great sense of smell have led to his being used for finding and rescuing missing persons. St Bernards were first bred by monks in the Swiss Alps just over 300 years ago, and soon became adept at tracking lost travellers, a job for which a

few of these are still used to this day.

The use of dogs for searching has developed greatly in recent years, with a large increase in the numbers of police and army dogs. It is interesting that a limited number of breeds has been selected for these functions, notably the German Shepherd dog, but also the Labrador Retriever and the Doberman Pinscher.

The German Shepherd dog has become the work dog of the twentieth century, adapting itself to a whole range of roles, from tracking and attack training, to guarding property and special training for demonstration shows. It seems that the use of dogs by the police and army, as well as mountain rescue organizations, is the fastest growing use of dogs in a genuine work role today. This is likely to continue with the upsurge in the training of dogs to sniff out drugs and explosives.

Opposite top Newfoundlands were used for sea rescue in the past. **Opposite bottom** For centuries Eskimos have depended on the Husky for survival. Dogs assist police and soldiers in many ways.
Top Sniffing out explosives.
Bottom Apprehending a criminal.

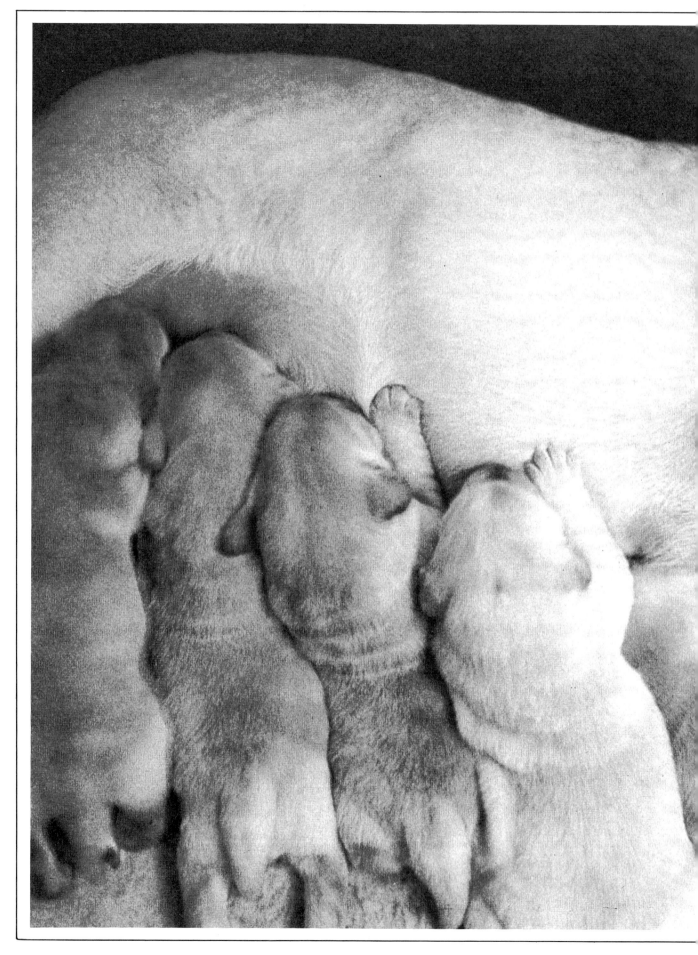

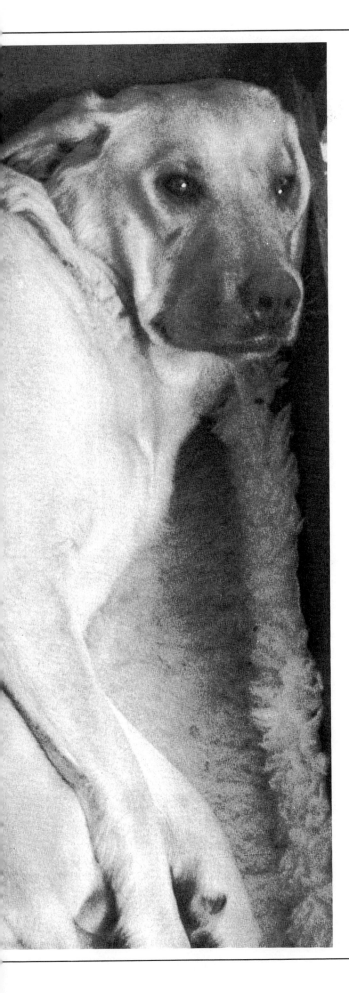

The dog's life-cycle

The dog will display interesting and unusual behaviour at different periods in its life-cycle, during courtship, mating and pregnancy. The courting rituals and nesting behaviour, when the pregnant bitch may tear up material to line her nest or carry toys about, are good examples of this. Once the pups are born, they enter a crucial period, as their adult behaviour can be radically influenced by their environment and early contact with other dogs and people.

Left A Labrador Retriever suckles her young. Unlike many species, the pups do not show teat preferences from one meal to the next.

Courtship rituals

After the resting phase when the bitch will not accept a mate, she comes into heat and courting begins. The dogs meet, nose to nose.

During the courtship ritual, the dogs will sniff each other's inguinal region, as two dogs meeting do, but with much greater interest.

Generally a period of play will follow, especially in the early days of heat, and the female will display the 'female standing posture'.

Once they are mature, male dogs are in a continuous state of readiness for courtship and mating. On the other hand, in female dogs such readiness is cyclical, meaning that the bitch is only sexually active periodically when she is 'in heat', or in scientific terms 'in oestrus'. On average a bitch comes in heat every six months, although the time between heats can vary from four to twelve months.

The behaviour of the male is largely dictated by the sexual status and behaviour of the bitch. She goes through a series of four distinct phases during her reproductive cycle. The longest phase is generally the quiet period when she will not accept a mate, and a male is unlikely to make any approach to her. This lasts on average for about four months, and during this time the reproductive organs are in what can be described as a resting state.

This resting phase is broken when the bitch starts to attract male dogs and, though she may show increased interest in them, she will still not allow mating. Her behaviour may change in other ways as well, for example she may become more excitable, lose her appetite and urinate more frequently.

This stage of the cycle can also be detected by anatomical changes in the vulva, or external genitalia, which swells and releases a bloody discharge. The bitch also releases a chemical compound in her urine which attracts male dogs, and may cause several to congregate around her home. This may irritate her owner, but little can be done to mask the odour. While most bitches show some or all of these

The male dog becomes attracted to the female at the stage in her cycle when physiological changes cause a discharge to be released, but she will not allow mating until she is in heat.

signs, there are sometimes no indications whatever, although there can still be a successful, if unwanted, mating.

Although males are attracted to a bitch in this state, and great interest is shown by the male if he is allowed to be with her, the bitch will almost never accept a male that attempts to mount her at this stage. Generally she will either walk away, or threaten the male which normally discourages him from being too persistent. This stage of the bitch's sexual cycle can vary in length from two to fifteen days, with an average of about six days being usual.

The next stage of the cycle is the period of heat, when the bitch is sexually receptive and successful fertilization can take place. There is usually a dramatic change in the behaviour of the bitch when heat begins. Whereas before she would reject the advances of males, she now does this less often and starts to display the characteristic posture known as female standing, where she stands with her vulval region presented to the male and her tail skewed to one side.

The eggs are generally shed on about the third day of heat, but the bitch will continue to accept advances for a week or more afterwards. It is quite possible for different members of a litter to be sired by two different males if more than one mating takes place.

Mating

When a male dog is allowed to meet a bitch in heat, the two of them will act out a courtship ritual, a sequence of actions which usually follows a similar pattern. First, they will greet each other by sniffing at the nose and then at the inguinal region, in much the same way as any two dogs meeting, although their interest in each other will be more intense than on a casual meeting, in particular on the part of the male. This frequently leads to a period of play, especially in the early days of heat. As a final display before mating, the male will often stand alertly alongside the bitch, facing in the same direction with his head and tail erect.

Assuming she is willing, the bitch will then stand in the presentation posture already described, and the male will mount. After mating has finished the male dismounts, but they remain joined by what is called a genital lock or tie. This can last anything from a few minutes up to an hour, and generally the dog and bitch stand quietly facing away from each other during this time. Sometimes the bitch in particular may become active, and even try to bite the male; if this happens, she should be quietened down.

This courtship sequence does not always go smoothly. Experience certainly plays an important part; inexperienced males may find mounting awkward and may initially try from the front or side. Also the build up to mating is generally much longer when one of the partners is inexperienced.

Individual preference can also have an affect. While dogs

Care should be taken to select a suitable mate, to complement the size, colouring and temperament of the bitch.

After a variable length of courting, the bitch will stand, her tail slightly to one side, to allow the male to mount.

The male mounts the bitch and mating occurs. This lasts just a few minutes, and then the male dismounts.

They then remain standing quietly facing away from each other, joined by the genital lock, which can last up to an hour.

do not form permanent pair bonds, studies have shown that females certainly have sexual preferences, and males also, but to a lesser extent. The degree of socialization of the dogs towards other dogs and towards people also plays a part, and of course any kind of disturbance in the vicinity can upset things.

The bitch is almost always brought to the stud male, rather than vice versa. This is because, being highly territorial and needing to take a dominant role during courtship and mating, the male performs much better on his home territory than in strange surroundings. The female, as the less dominant and less active partner, is less affected by the surroundings.

Once her period of heat is over, the bitch quickly ceases to be sexually attractive to the male, and at the same time she refuses any sexual advances he might make. This behaviour change is usually rapid, but she may refuse a male one day and accept him the next. If there has been no mating or if it has not been successful, the bitch will return to a sexually inactive state for some months.

The various forms of sexual activity disappear immediately in bitches that are spayed, and rapidly, although not necessarily immediately, following castration in males. Veterinary surgeons can now give injections which will postpone, but not prevent, a bitch's coming in heat.

The pregnant dog

The bitch may act strangely during her pregnancy – perhaps carrying toys around, and even trying to curl around them as if they were puppies. The owner should be tolerant of odd behaviour at this time, only worrying if it continues after the pups leave.

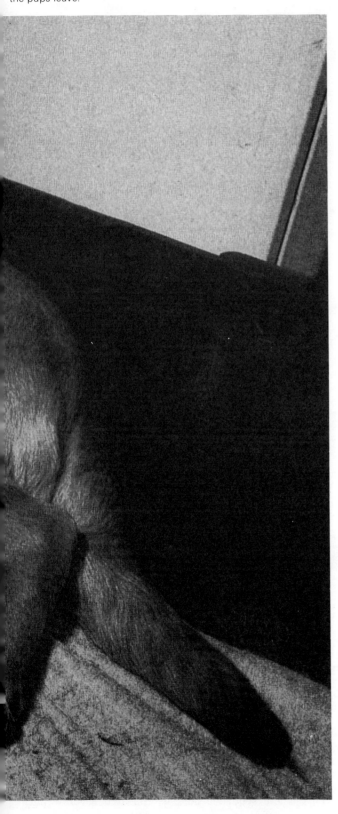

When a bitch has been successfully mated, the pregnancy that ensues lasts about 63 days, although there can be a variation of several days in either direction. At the start of the pregnancy, there is nothing obvious in terms of appearance or behaviour to distinguish a pregnant bitch. A veterinarian may be able to detect the presence of puppies in the bitch's abdomen about three weeks after mating, but outwardly there is no change at this time.

At about five weeks the owner may be able to see that the bitch is pregnant, from a slight increase in her bodyweight and a distention of the abdomen. Depending on the individual, this may not be recognized until six or seven weeks. The bitch then increases in size and weight rapidly up until full term at nine weeks.

A common phenomenon in dogs is a state known as pseudo, or false, pregnancy; this often occurs after a mating that has been infertile. The external characteristics of false pregnancy are extremely similar to those of a real pregnancy, but there are no pups developing in the womb. However, the bitch may show signs of abdominal swelling and also it is a characteristic of bitches during their first pregnancy, whether false or genuine, that the teats become erect and enlarge to two or three times.

A false pregnancy sometimes ends well before the full nine weeks of a normal pregnancy; the abdomen will suddenly reduce in size and the bitch no longer appears pregnant. However, in other instances, a number of behaviour changes characteristic of pregnant bitches near full term may be observed.

Near to term, a bitch will generally become restless and may roam around the house as if looking for something. She may make whining or crying noises, and tear up any available material for nest building. Sometimes she may fail to respond to obedience commands.

The owner should make a few special considerations for a pregnant bitch. It is important to provide extra food from the fourth week of pregnancy working up to two or three times the normal amount by full term. A suitable site for whelping should be prepared, perhaps a special box. Finally, if the bitch does behave strangely during her pregnancy, the owner should be tolerant.

Providing a whelping box

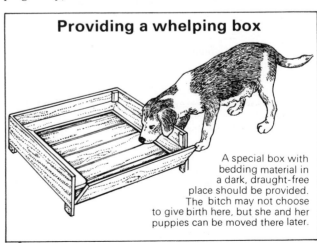

A special box with bedding material in a dark, draught-free place should be provided. The bitch may not choose to give birth here, but she and her puppies can be moved there later.

Birth

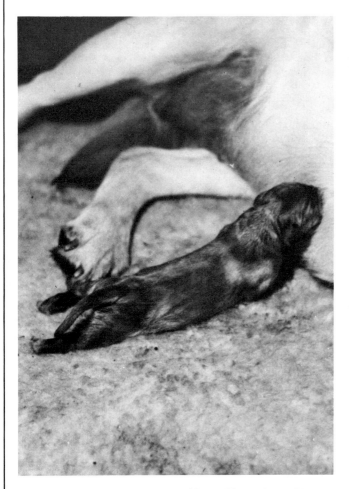

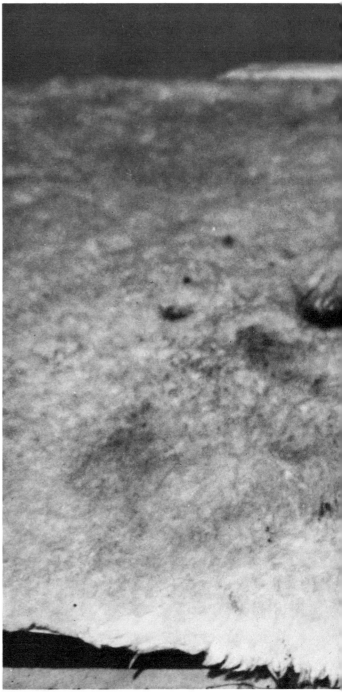

Above The mother will burst the sac around the pup and lick it clean, stimulating it to breathe. Soon it will crawl around and start to suckle. She will attend to each newborn immediately, making sure that none of them escape from the nest, **right**.

The first signs of an imminent birth are an increase in the bitch's activity and a decrease in her appetite. There is much variation between individuals, but generally this activity becomes more intense somewhere between 12 and 24 hours before labour starts. Another sign of imminent labour is a decline of body temperature from the normal 101.5°F to 98°F. Sometimes labour can begin quite unexpectedly.

Immediately prior to labour the bitch will usually devote a lot of time to trying to build a nest. If she is given newspaper or rags, these will be shredded and frequently rearranged around her. If there is no nesting material of this kind available, she is likely to paw at the sides of her chosen box or nesting area. She may become increasingly aggressive towards strangers as labour approaches, but increasingly friendly towards her owner.

During labour the mother generally lies on her side in her chosen basket or box, facing outwards with her back to the wall. Her breathing may become very rapid at times, alternating with periods of slower, deeper breathing, and sometimes she may breathe normally for a spell. During labour itself, the hindlegs often twitch and the whole body may shiver.

Bitches generally whelp lying down, but they sometimes stand up and move around while straining. Strong uterine contractions follow, and with the straining of other muscles, these cause the expulsion of the pup. The foetal membranes and afterbirth are expelled after a further series of contractions.

This whole sequence may be repeated several times

depending on the number of puppies. The puppies are born at irregular intervals, generally about 20 to 60 minutes apart. Longer delays can be caused by disturbances, especially if other dogs intrude, but also if people interfere. Disturbances of this kind can also interrupt the normal contraction sequence during labour.

After the birth of the first pup and each succeeding one, the mother will attend to the newborn at once, removing the sac enclosing it and vigorously licking it all over. This licking should stimulate the pup to breathe, and it may even cry out. The mother will then bite through the umbilical cord, and eat the afterbirth and that part of the cord still attached to it. This may look unpleasant, but it is quite normal, not just for dogs, but for almost all wild animals.

In general, a bitch will have no serious problems with whelping, and any attempts to help her are more likely to cause trouble than to prove beneficial. Breech presentations are perfectly normal in dogs and are not a cause for concern. However, there can be difficulties with some breeds, particularly the toy ones. It is a good idea therefore if the owner is on hand to give minor assistance if this proves necessary, and to call a vet in an emergency.

A suitable whelping box is a useful aid to a successful birth, and it is sensible to familiarize the bitch with it beforehand. It is a good idea to have a protective shelf on the inner wall; this will help to prevent the pups being crushed inadvertently by the mother during the first few days. If any pups do die, or are stillborn, the mother will continue to lick and care for them while they are warm, but will ignore them once they become cold.

The newborn pup

A puppy is born at a very early stage in its development, although after birth it grows and gains control of its senses extremely rapidly. At birth its eyes are closed so it is unable to see; its ears are not sufficiently developed for it to be able to hear; nor, it is thought, can it smell anything. The newborn puppy does have a primitive sense of taste, but at this early stage it relies almost entirely on its sense of touch and its sensitivity to cold.

The newborn pup's behaviour is almost equally restricted, but it is highly functional. As long as the conditions are suitable, the pup spends 90 per cent of its time sleeping and most of the rest feeding. The pup is able to go straight from a period of wakefulness to being asleep with no apparent signs of drowsiness in between.

During its wakeful periods, the young pup spends its time either searching for a teat to feed from, or else simply suckling. Pups normally move about by sliding along on their stomachs making swimming-type movements with their front legs. At the same time, their heads swing from side to side in their search for a warm object. If a pup fails to make contact with its mother after travelling a short distance, it will set off in the same manner in a new direction. Once it touches the mother's body, the pup will move along parallel with it until it contacts a suitable area,

where it will burrow in and come to rest once its head and shoulders are covered. It will behave in the same way if offered a human hand.

After a few minutes, the pup will make further exploratory movements in order to find a teat; when it finds one, it may not begin to suckle for some time, although there soon ceases to be any delay as the pup becomes practised. Unlike kittens, pups do not appear to prefer one particular nipple. Although the sense of taste is poorly developed, pups will turn away from any bitter substance, while milk, on the other hand, does seem to appeal to them.

Newborn pups have a reflex which makes them withdraw any limb which encounters something painful. If a pup finds himself away from his mother in a cold place, he becomes restless, more alert than usual and his breathing becomes more rapid; he will also make a distress call comparable to human crying, which is usually termed 'mewing'. Some studies have revealed the strange fact that a mother will often ignore this mewing, and may even squash a pup that is crying in distress. However, if she can see a pup moving around some distance away, she will bring it back to the nest, but not if she merely hears it. Pups also make a grunting noise, which appears to indicate pleasure when distress is relieved.

Starting to grow

The pup's development is at its most rapid during the first four weeks of its life. By then it may weigh as much as seven times its birthweight, and its abilities to see, smell and move around, will have progressed enormously. The time spent sleeping will rapidly decrease, and the pup will begin to enjoy a range of other activities.

Vision develops extremely quickly, so that by four weeks of age the puppy's eyesight is almost as good as that of an adult dog. At birth the eyelids are closed, and the light sensitive region of the eye, the retina, is poorly developed, although the puppy will react if a bright light is shone through its retina.

When the puppy is between 10 and 15 days old, his eyelids open, but he still cannot see well, and responds inconsistently to lights or moving objects. By the time he is four weeks old, the pup will follow a moving object with his eyes in the same way as an adult dog. However, the brain is still not fully developed; for example, the pup seems unable to recognize its mother until about a week later.

The development of hearing follows a similar time pattern to that of vision. The ear canal opens when the puppy is about two weeks old, and full hearing has developed by four or five weeks. General development of the brain, such skills as coordination of limb and head movements, walking and responses to touch, occur at the same time, so that by the time he is five weeks old the puppy

Below The newborn pups are totally dependent on their mother for food and warmth, but change rapidly in the first four weeks from their primitive state at birth. Faculties begin to develop, the pup will start to sleep less, and will be very active by six weeks.

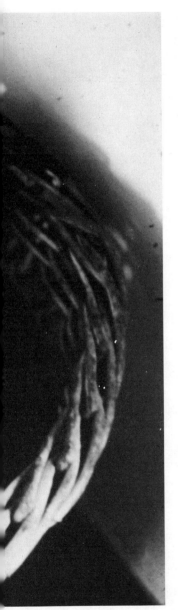

The first few weeks: beginning to explore

Three days old. Unable to see, hear or smell, the newborn pup relies on its sense of touch, feeding every two hours, sleeping in between.

One week old. The puppy will crawl about the nest, searching for the teat, and thus burrowing into anything soft and warm, even a human hand

Two weeks old. The pup is starting to become more active. The eyes are now open, although they are not yet fully able to see.

Four weeks. Sense of hearing and smell have developed to some extent. Eyes can follow a moving object. Starts playful fighting with other pups.

Five to six weeks. The facial muscles have developed; the puppy now has a full repertoire of expressions, important for communication.

is ready to learn all the other abilities needed for adult life.

While the puppy is developing all these skills and capabilities, its range of experience remains fairly limited. Puppies continue to spend most of their time sleeping or feeding, and when sleeping they arrange themselves in a pile for warmth. When one wakes up, its movements will wake the others and all will tend to feed together.

Puppies are not able to pass waste matter or urine without being stimulated to do so. The mother generally does this by licking the pups, which causes reflex elimination. She does this for the first two to three weeks, and also ingests all the waste matter, thereby keeping the nest clean. After this time, the pups will eliminate of their own

accord, and will usually leave the immediate area of the nest to do so.

Puppies will start to eat solid or semi-solid food when they are about three weeks old. They will eat anything they find in the nest box, and occasionally the may stimulate their mother to regurgitate food for them, by licking at her face and mouth. It is quite normal for wolf mothers to feed their young in this way.

At four or five weeks the puppies are ready to start playing, exploring and interacting fully with each other. It is interesting that by this time, five weeks, the facial muscles have developed fully to give the puppy its full repertoire of expressions.

Social development

These dogs socialize easily with other animals, **below left**, and people, **below right**, unlike pups taken too early or late from the litter. The critical socialization period in the pup's development is from about five to twelve weeks.

Unlike cats, dogs are naturally social animals. Studies have established that there is a critical period during a puppy's development when it must have contact with both people and other dogs, if it is to develop normally into an adult pet. This period starts as early as about three and a half weeks, when puppies start to play with each other, and continues until about 12 weeks, after which the social attitude of the puppy towards its own and other species has become relatively fixed.

In the wild, the importance of this period appears to be that it is the time when individuals learn to interact with other members of their own species; they learn principally about the dominant and subordinate relationships that are important in maintaining the stability of a dog pack, and they learn to recognize their own species.

The importance of this socialization period in producing a good house pet has been shown by several studies. Puppies that have little or no contact with humans until they are three months old generally make poor pets. They are usually timid and afraid of people, and do not develop the dependency on the owner that most pet dogs show. Research into the training of guide dogs has shown that puppies remaining with their mothers beyond 12 weeks are not suitable for such training, and it is only with intensive training that such dogs can become acceptable house pets.

The best age for a dog to begin to interact with people seems to be between six and eight weeks, and this is therefore the best age at which to buy a puppy and bring it into the house.

A puppy which is taken away from its mother too early, at four or five weeks, and then reared exclusively with people, may develop different problems. It can become excessively attached to its owner, and when it matures it may show a lack of sexual interest in other dogs.

The socialization period is also the best time to acquaint a puppy with other types of pet. Experiments have been conducted where puppies have been raised alone with rabbits or cats; the result was that they preferred to be with these species rather than their own, at least in the short term. A puppy raised in the presence of a cat, rabbit or guinea pig will readily accept their company.

Caring for your dog

The choice of the right puppy for the owner's circumstances is vital, if a happy relationship between man and dog is to be created. The dog will be part of the household for many years, and the owner must take responsibility for the things which help keep a dog happy and healthy — grooming, excercise and correct nutrition. Like any human, the dog requires a changing diet as it grows from puppyhood to maturity, has a tendency to put on weight if overfed, and needs special care in old age.

Left Some breeds, such as this Cocker Spaniel, need special attention. Long ears are prone to infections and must be checked regularly.

Choosing a pup

Choosing a pup is almost certainly the most important decision regarding his pet, that an owner ever makes; the individual that is selected will be his responsibility for many years to come. A host of considerations affect this choice; the size of home and garden, the size of the dog, the facilities for exercise, personal preferences regarding breeds, the choice available, the health of the available puppies, the desire for pedigree or non-pedigree, the preferred sex, and the behaviour of the puppies in the chosen litter.

Many of these decisions are matters of common sense, for example whether there is enough room for a given size of dog, although a surprising number of owners make mistakes over this; hence the need for welfare organizations to look after abandoned pets. However, the puppy's behaviour is vitally important, and here there are a number of considerations, which often pass unnoticed by even the most considerate of owners.

The temperament of a dog is crucial and depends on many factors. One of these is certainly its parentage, so at least the mother, and if possible the father, should be seen and their temperament assessed. The future behaviour of the dog is strongly influenced by the age at which the puppy is purchased and brought into the owner's home. The importance of the socialization period has already been stressed, and it is clear that around seven or eight weeks is the best age at which to obtain a new puppy. Certainly they must be purchased somewhere between six and thirteen weeks. The puppy will then become fully socialized towards the owner with sufficient, but not too great, socialization towards other dogs. Any puppy kept with other dogs for more than his first thirteen weeks is likely to be almost untrainable as a pet.

A puppy who is purchased early is less likely to be disturbed by the sudden change of surroundings. Puppies become familiar with surroundings as they get older; a change from, say, a kennel to a house with children may be traumatic to an older puppy, while a younger one would merely explore and show interest.

Once a suitable litter of pups from which to choose has been found, the individuals must be considered, as their personalities will be different. The first choice to make is between a bitch and a dog. A dog is likely to be more assertive and need firmer handling, and there may be problems from straying or urination indoors. A bitch, on the other hand, will come into heat twice a year and so will need special attention at these times and there is still some risk of unwanted puppies.

As well as the sex differences, an examination of the litter is likely to reveal that some puppies are more pugnacious and come forward to meet a human inquirer, and perhaps start play fighting with another pup. Others may appear quiet or fearful and stay in their box away from humans.

There is unlikely to be one best dog in any litter, because differences in human personality mean that different dogs appeal to, and suit, different people. For example, a bold assertive dog would not suit a quiet, elderly person living alone; similarly a quiet bitch might not suit an outgoing person with a forceful personality.

It is best to try and judge the potential character and degree of dominance of a young puppy, and then relate this to the character of the owner. It is obviously difficult to make judgements of this kind for either party, but it is certainly worthwhile studying a group of puppies for a time and attempting to assess something of their character in terms of fearfulness, friendliness, alertness, activity and dominance.

Right and opposite The choice of a pup is a crucial one, and future owners should not be hasty in making a decision – the dog will be part of the household for many years to come. The pup should be healthy and of a suitable size, breed and temperament for its new home and owner.

Care and attention

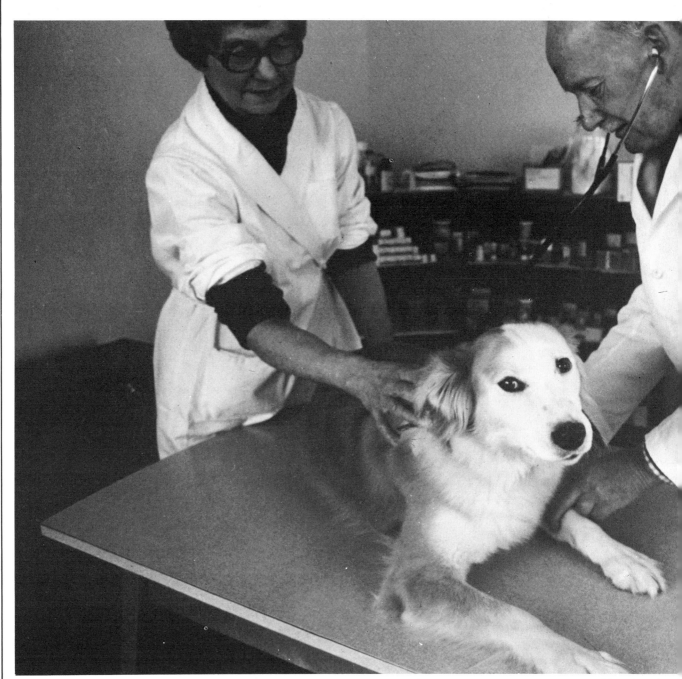

An owner takes on considerable responsibility when he acquires a dog. Careful consideration should be given to what care the dog will require, the cost, future holidays, absences from home, and the likely lifespan of the dog. Unlike most other purchases which can be resold or discarded, a dog must be viewed as forming part of the family for at least ten years, although of course during that time he will give back unquestioning love and devotion in return for all the care lavished on him by his owners.

The first few days when a puppy, or an older dog, is brought into the home are of immense importance, because this is the foundation on which its future happiness will be based. Planning and forethought are necessary before the arrival, so that all is ready. Any new puppy away from its mother, littermates and familiar surroundings for the first time is bound to be frightened. It should be given a dark box or basket in which it can shelter, a toy to chew on, and little fuss should be made of it in case it becomes frightened.

Below At some time the dog may require medical attention, necessitating a visit to the vet, seen here giving a routine examination. Dogs should be attended to as soon as they appear unwell and, like human patients, they need quiet, care and consideration.

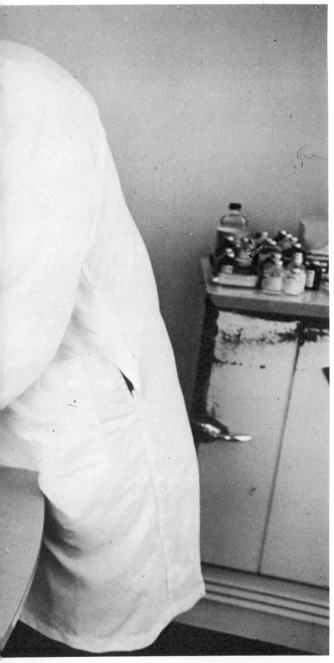

Collars and leads for different activities

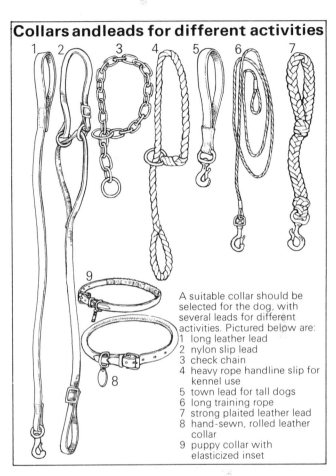

A suitable collar should be selected for the dog, with several leads for different activities. Pictured below are:
1 long leather lead
2 nylon slip lead
3 check chain
4 heavy rope handline slip for kennel use
5 town lead for tall dogs
6 long training rope
7 strong plaited leather lead
8 hand-sewn, rolled leather collar
9 puppy collar with elasticized inset

It is a mistake to bring a puppy into the house at Christmas time. There will be much more activity than usual, less time to devote to the puppy, and the child for whom the pup has been bought will have too many other distractions. The puppy is more likely to be seen as a short term toy than a living animal that will need care and attention for many years.

Vaccinations are necessary at about the time a puppy first enters the home. At twelve weeks, or earlier, vac-cinations should be given against four diseases: distemper, hepatitis, jaundice and nephritis. Some of these may have been given while the puppy was with the breeder, and this should be checked. A worming preparation should also be given at this time. Puppies, more than adult dogs, are liable to pass worms in their faeces, but worming should be continued, even when they are older, and is especially important for the pregnant bitch.

In most countries of the world – the United Kingdom is an exception because the disease is not endemic there – dogs are given rabies vaccinations annually, and this is usually compulsory by law. The disease can be passed on to humans by an infected dog, and unless treated quickly can cause death. It is therefore inadvisable to play with a strange dog in an infected country because, while the classic view of a rabid dog is that it is mad and foaming at the mouth, the disease more frequently manifests itself in a quieter form.

Many other diseases can affect dogs. A veterinary surgeon should be consulted as soon as a dog appears unwell; any delay may make the condition worse, and perhaps more expensive to cure. The cost of treatment is an important consideration for potential dog owners, as dogs may require medical attention at some point.

Left All dogs enjoy periods of play and regular exercise, which benefit them both physically and psychologically.

Exercise and grooming

Unlike cats which gain enough exercise by their own endeavours, dogs usually need to be exercised by their owners. By nature dogs are built for stamina and travelling long distances and, as a species, they have a tendency towards obesity. Cats, on the other hand, are designed for short, fast bursts of movement and they regulate their own body weight quite effectively. In dogs, lack of sufficient exercise may even contribute to disease of the heart and arteries, in the same way as it is thought to in humans.

Some dogs can get sufficient exercise without troubling their owners, if they have a large enough garden to run around in. By themselves, they are unlikely to run enough, but the presence of another dog will lead to play and chasing games which will give both dogs plenty of exercise.

For most dogs, however, a walk with the owner is the principal source of exercise. The length of the walk required depends on the breed, but is roughly proportional to the size of the dog. For the owner the walk need not be so long, if the dog can be exercised off the lead. A dog that can rush around on its own will probably cover three times the distance its owner walks. A hard run uses up several times more energy than a slow walk over the same distance, so it is difficult to say exactly how far a dog needs to go each day. Even the smallest toy breeds need at least half a mile or so each day, but for the largest breeds several miles is probably ideal. As a dog grows old, less walking is needed but exercise should never stop.

Apart from exercise and feeding, dogs should have their coats groomed regularly. For short-haired dogs, daily grooming is not necessary, but occasional grooming does improve the appearance of the coat. Daily grooming may well be best, however, for long-haired breeds. This should begin when the dog is still a puppy, so that it becomes part of a standard routine to which the dog will not object.

Grooming helps to prevent the coat matting, gives it a shine, and also removes excess hair, reducing the amount shed on furniture and carpets. The length and type of coat will determine which combs and brushes should be used. While grooming a dog, it is a good idea to look out for parasites, such as fleas and lice, so that immediate treatment can be given.

Dogs need to be bathed and shampooed at least occasionally. Again, it is sensible to introduce the idea of bathing while the dog is still a young puppy, so that it is not frightened as an adult.

A dog's claws, which are really part of the skin, grow in the same way as hair does and may therefore need regular treatment. Trimming is best done little and often; if the dew claw has not been removed, it will need a lot of trimming because it will not wear down as it grows, unlike the other claws.

Centre Exercise is very important for dogs, who benefit from the stimulation of people or other dogs, making them run around more.

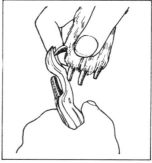

Long nails can cause problems, so should be carefully trimmed.

Long hair needs grooming daily, to avoid matting.

All dogs should be groomed to keep the coat in a good, healthy condition. Some dogs, such as the poodle, need special clipping every 6–8 weeks, as they do not moult. Scissors or electric clippers can be used for this.

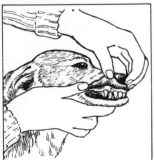

Calculus may build up on teeth. Chewing bones can prevent this.

Ears should be inspected and wiped gently, but not probed.

When bathing the dog, avoid getting soap in eyes and ears.

Dry with a large towel after the dog has shaken itself.

Cars and kennels

Most dogs are likely to travel fairly frequently in cars. The vaccinations already mentioned will necessitate a visit to the veterinarian, and in many cases this will be by car. Unfortunately treatment at the veterinarian's will almost always give some discomfort to the dog, and this can make any visit after the first one a fairly traumatic event, once the dog senses where it is going. If the dog's first car journey is to the vet, this may make him frightened of all car travel by a process of association. It is therefore worth thinking ahead, and perhaps giving the puppy a brief ride to a place he will like, such as a park, before the first visit to the vet.

Some dogs dislike car journeys for other reasons. Travel sickness affects some dogs, as it does some people, and the reason is the same, the influence of the car's movements on the balance organs. On the other hand, many dogs enjoy car rides immensely. Most of them regard the car as an extension of their own home territory and may bark at any strange person that approaches when they are left alone in the car.

It is not good for the dog to stick its head out of the window while the car is moving. Not only is there a danger of it hitting something, but also the fast flow of air can dry out the eyes, causing irritation. When the car is parked and the dog is left inside, it should be in the shade and a window should be left open a few inches to provide air.

Dogs are very dependent animals, and are unhappy even when their owners are absent for short periods. Any

Right Adequate ventilation and, in hot weather, water and shade, should be provided for the dog left in a car. A familiar toy may ease the trauma of time spent in a boarding kennel, such as above.

potential owner who is at work daily with no one else in the house should think carefully before buying a dog. When left alone, dogs become bored and sometimes destructive.

If the owner is to be away from home for a period of days or weeks, the dog may need to be boarded in a kennel. Here he will not suffer from loneliness in one sense, because he will at least be in the company of other dogs. Nevertheless, the change in surroundings, the low level of human contact, and the absence of the owner can have a psychological effect on the dog. Most dogs cope with a kennel for two or three weeks very well, but it is probably a good idea to leave a familiar toy at the kennels and if possible the dog's normal food, although it may eat less than usual.

Some kennels are not just for boarding, but act as sanctuaries for stray and unwanted dogs. Many people prefer to acquire one of these instead of buying a young puppy, because these unfortunate dogs are in great need of a home. Dogs of this kind are likely to present more problems than a puppy because their characters are already formed. Also they may have been mistreated, and being older are less adaptable and less easy to train. However, with love and patience, many such dogs can become excellent house pets – no different from those reared in one home since they were puppies. The quiet, planned introduction into the new home, and the necessary basic training should be just the same as for any younger dog. However, it may well take longer for the dog to become a fully socialized member of the family.

The ageing process

It is often said that one year of a man's life is equivalent to about seven of a dog's. In one sense this is true since the average lifespan of a dog is around ten years as against a man's 70. In other ways the comparison is rather misleading, since a few dogs will live to 15 or even 20 years, the 'equivalent' of which no human ever reaches. On the other hand, certain breeds such as the Great Dane and the Irish Wolfhound have a comparatively short average lifespan, perhaps only six or seven years. No one is certain why dogs age so much more quickly than people, and one of the questions that puzzles biologists is why the various diseases of senility should occur so much earlier in dogs.

The commonest causes of death, however, are not quite the same for dogs as for people. Dogs show a much higher susceptibility to accidents than people, particularly road accidents. This is because a dog never learns as well as a person how to respond to traffic, and they are also much more likely to be distracted and suddenly rush into danger.

As dogs get older, a number of changes take place. Their stamina is reduced and they start to exercise less. This, combined with a general reduction in metabolic rate, means that they need less food as they get older. This should be watched carefully, and rations should be reduced as soon as an elderly dog shows signs of putting on weight. The protein requirement will also fall, and those dogs that develop kidney problems may need a special low protein diet.

In many ways the diseases of dogs in old age are similar to those of humans. They can develop cancers; may have heart trouble or other problems of the circulatory system, and they may also suffer from a range of other age-related diseases. Especially common are problems with the eyes and with the joints. The latter seem particularly severe, because a disabled dog is an especially sad sight. Some joint problems, in particular patellar luxation which affects the forelimbs and hip dysplasia which attacks the hind-limbs, are proportionately more common in certain breeds. These diseases seem to have a strong genetic component, as do some other afflictions, including eye problems and even some behavioural illnesses such as epilepsy.

Of course it is not possible to halt old age in a dog, but much can be done to keep the dog happy. The continuing of established routines can be very beneficial, and it should be remembered that in old age some behaviour problems can be triggered by a sudden change in circumstances, such as moving house or introduction to active young children.

Two of the most difficult things to face are the question of when it is kindest to put a dog down, and then the period of bereavement that follows. The death may be especially difficult for children but, despite the sadness, this can help to teach them about death, and in turn will help them cope later with the death of a relative. If a well loved pet is replaced by a young puppy, this helps to demonstrate the continuity of life and bring happiness back to the household. The love for the former dog will quickly be transferred, and this is true not just for children but for adults too, because replacement of a favourite dog at a later date is always more difficult.

Similar physical changes take place in both dogs and humans as they age, with a gradual loss of energy, hearing and so on. **Above and right** The young dog is trim and alert-looking, with a good, thick coat and dark pigmentation of the nose.

Left and above In the middle years, there will be some signs of the ageing process. The dog will become less lively, and may tend to put on weight. The first white hairs will start to show on dark breeds.

Left and above The skin of the older dog loosens up and becomes less elastic. There will be a lot of white hair on the face, and the nose turns pinker, due to loss of the ability to synthesize melanin, associated with the greying process in humans. The tendency to put on weight increases.

Hide and seek

The feeding habits of dogs are as varied as those of humans. Some dogs will eat almost anything they can get hold of, including books, toys and other inedible objects. Others are extremely particular about what they eat, and their owners have great problems finding foods that will consistently please their pets. Yet other dogs have very strange individual preferences for such foods as bananas, salads, or potatoes, but in other respects they will eat quite normally.

Compared with its wild relatives, the domestic dog has an easy time finding its food. The wild members of the family are essentially carnivores, eating principally mammals ranging from mice up to large deer. However, in some regions and at certain times of the year the wild members of the dog family can be much more omnivorous. In suburbs of English towns the red fox may subsist largely on earthworms at certain times of the year. Also, during times of hardship, several wild canid species including the wolf will turn to vegetable matter, especially berries, to supplement their diet; if times are especially bad, this can become their main source of food.

It is held that most large carnivores eat only intermittently, and gorge themselves when they do catch something, but this does not apply to all members of the dog family. Those that eat small animals catch their prey and eat at intervals throughout the day, and even those that feed on large animals often return to eat at intervals after the initial killing.

Foxes will carry the food to be cached to a selected spot.

The food is held in the mouth while a shallow hole is dug.

Soil is replaced over the cache by long sweeps of the nose.

This suggests that the common belief that dogs should be fed only once a day, and even made to fast one day a week, is incorrect. Dogs can certainly thrive quite happily on such a regime, although the fasting element can upset a dog and lead to strange behaviour because he is expecting food which does not arrive. Dogs which are given continuous access to food which constitutes a complete diet, eat between about 8 and 25 small meals per day, depending on the individual. On this type of regime many dogs will eat only the food they require; others may get fat, but they are the ones who are likely to get fat on any regime.

If dogs do not eat all their food at once, they frequently cache what is left over; both wild and domestic dogs do this and the most common example of it is the burying of the bone. Any food which is surplus to immediate requirements is likely to be hidden where the dog can easily find it again. Unlike cats, most dogs seem prepared to eat meat that is high almost to the point of rotting.

Foxes have often been observed caching their food, carefully carrying it to a chosen spot where they dig a shallow hole, which is neatly covered with soil.

Although the dog is primarily a carnivore, he should strictly be classified as an omnivore, because he can, and often does, eat vegetable matter. It is this ability to be omnivorous that creates the big range of preferred diets among dogs. It also explains why most dogs are much less particular about what they will eat than cats which are true carnivores, eating only meat.

Below Like the fox and other species of wild dog, the domestic pet is often observed caching its surplus food. The dog will return to these hiding places, and chew on the old bones.

Overfeeding

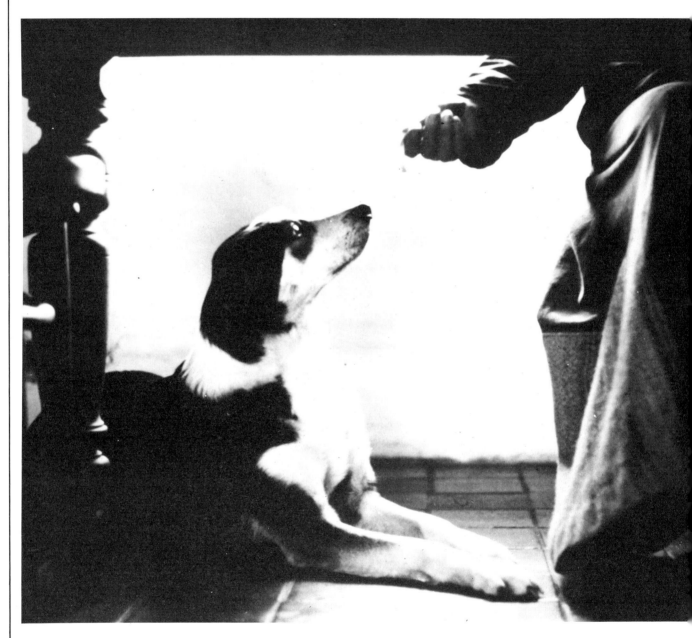

One of the commonest dietary problems with dogs is obesity, due to overeating; most estimates find that between 20 and 30 per cent of pet dogs suffer in this way. The likelihood of obesity varies from breed to breed; some, such as the Labrador and Cocker Spaniel, are commonly affected, while others, like the Red Setter and most of the Terriers, are much less susceptible.

Many factors can affect a dog's weight, but the simplest solution to obesity is to feed the dog less and make sure he is not getting food elsewhere. Sometimes there are medical causes, and if there is any suspicion of this, a veterinary surgeon should be consulted before a weight reduction programme is started.

Feeding the dog titbits at the table encourages him to eat more than he needs, and can lead to obesity and undesirable begging.

It is interesting to speculate as to why dogs should show such a high susceptibility to obesity. One dog's tendency to obesity may be the palatability of its food. Certainly a dog is likely to eat more than usual if he is given an especially tasty meal. However, in the long term most dogs cease to respond in this way and regulate their intake as before.

Another related factor is the social side of eating, what psychologists call social facilitation. Studies have revealed that puppies eat more if they feed in a group than if they are alone. This may still apply to adult dogs with the

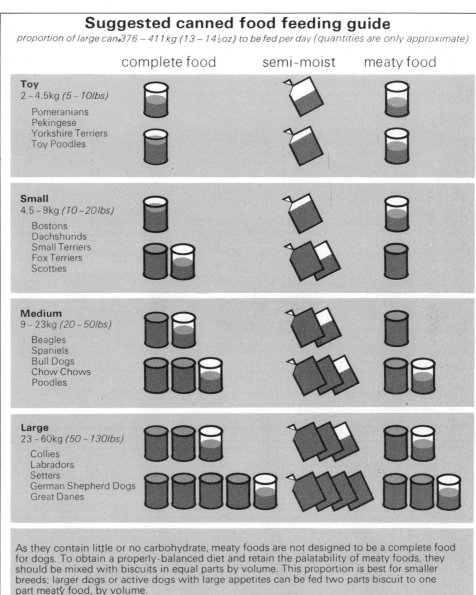

Suggested canned food feeding guide

proportion of large can 376 – 411kg (13 – 14½oz) to be fed per day (quantities are only approximate)

complete food   semi-moist   meaty food

Toy
2 – 4.5kg *(5 – 10lbs)*

Pomeranians
Pekingese
Yorkshire Terriers
Toy Poodles

Small
4.5 – 9kg *(10 – 20lbs)*

Bostons
Dachshunds
Small Terriers
Fox Terriers
Scotties

Medium
9 – 23kg *(20 – 50lbs)*

Beagles
Spaniels
Bull Dogs
Chow Chows
Poodles

Large
23 – 60kg *(50 – 130lbs)*

Collies
Labradors
Setters
German Shepherd Dogs
Great Danes

As they contain little or no carbohydrate, meaty foods are not designed to be a complete food for dogs. To obtain a properly-balanced diet and retain the palatability of meaty foods, they should be mixed with biscuits in equal parts by volume. This proportion is best for smaller breeds; larger dogs or active dogs with large appetites can be fed two parts biscuit to one part meaty food, by volume.

owner's mere presence encouraging a dog to eat more.

However, the majority of cases of obesity are almost certainly due to the dog's own weight control mechanism rather than to these external factors. For one thing, all breeds would show the same tendency to obesity if external factors were wholly to blame. On the whole the breeds which are most particular about their food – often the smaller ones – have fewer weight problems than the larger, often less choosy, breeds. It is also well established that the spaying of bitches and the castration of dogs both tend to increase the likelihood of obesity. It appears that the hormonal changes resulting from these operations in some way alter the mechanisms which regulate weight.

Age, exercise and the seasons also play a part; older dogs need less food than growing dogs or active young adults, and cold weather increases appetite so that some dogs may need more food than others.

A method of regulating a dog's weight that is often effective is to maintain the bulk of the diet while reducing the calories; the same principle is used with some human diet foods. Balanced diets of this kind can be obtained from veterinary surgeons. This is unlikely to fool the dog for long, because dogs, like humans, regulate their food intake by calories rather than bulk. This is also why a range of diets from complete dry and semi-moist to canned meat and fresh food are all acceptable to most dogs.

Growth and nutrition

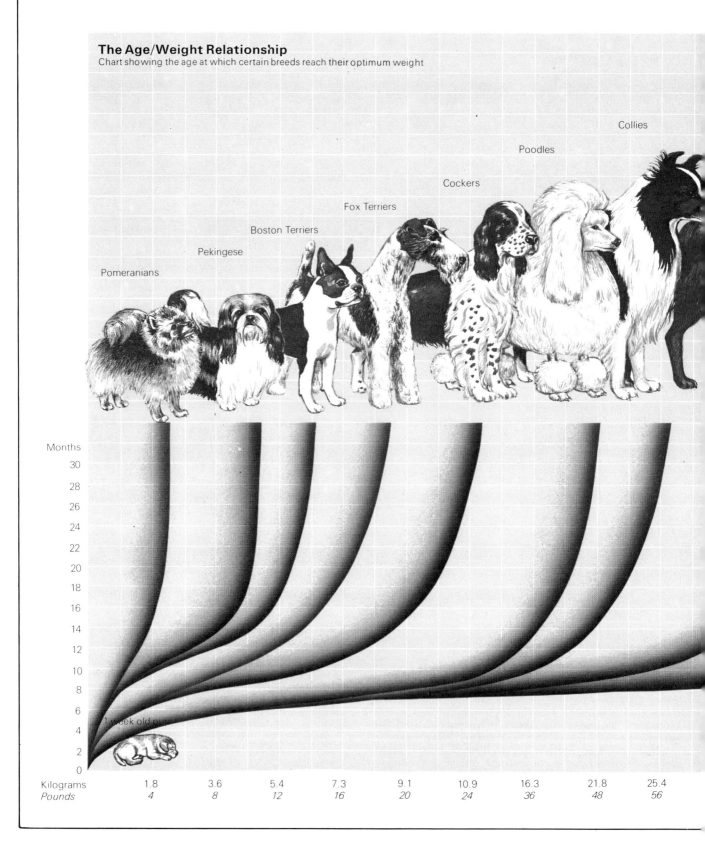

The Age/Weight Relationship
Chart showing the age at which certain breeds reach their optimum weight

Collies

Poodles

Cockers

Fox Terriers

Boston Terriers

Pekingese

Pomeranians

Months
30
28
26
24
22
20
18
16
14
12
10
8
6
4
2
0

1 week old pup

Kilograms	1.8	3.6	5.4	7.3	9.1	10.9	16.3	21.8	25.4
Pounds	*4*	*8*	*12*	*16*	*20*	*24*	*36*	*48*	*56*

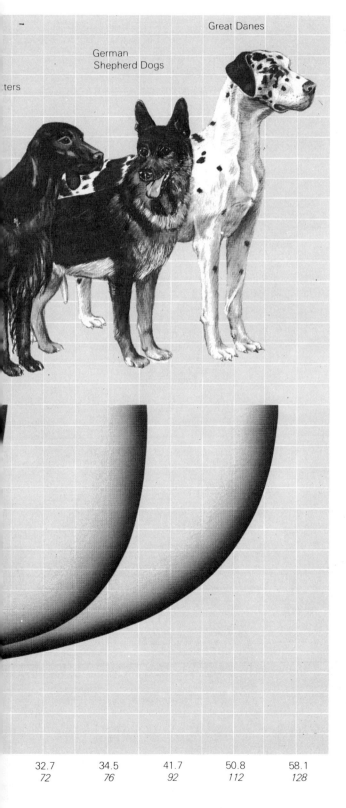

German
Shepherd Dogs

Great Danes

ters

| 32.7 | 34.5 | 41.7 | 50.8 | 58.1 |
| *72* | *76* | *92* | *112* | *128* |

Dogs have certainly been reported to eat, and apparently enjoy, a huge range of foods, some of which seem rather bizarre. Dogs are commonly seen eating grass; it is unlikely that they obtain more than a tiny amount of nutritional value from this because their digestive system is not equipped to cope with it. Nor is it likely that dogs eat grass for vitamins, since, unlike humans, they do not have to take in vitamin C because they make it in their body. Most frequently dogs eat grass because it acts as an emetic, making them vomit; this is desirable if, for example, the stomach contains indigestible fur or bones.

The partially omnivorous nature of the dog's diet is probably why the dog needs less protein in its diet than the cat. Like all other animals the dog requires a mixture of carbohydrates, fats and proteins. These all supply energy, and protein is also required for body building. Certain important minerals, such as calcium for bones and salt for body fluids, are also required. Other minerals and vitamins are necessary for specialized functions within the body; for example, the red blood cells depend on iron.

Wild dogs obtain all these substances from their naturally varied diet. Pet dogs can be given the right nourishment in a number of ways. Most convenient are specially prepared pet foods which are carefully balanced by the manufacturers to provide the right nutrients in the correct proportions. Cooked meat or offal with biscuits is also quite satisfactory, but it is all too easy to supply insufficient calcium. Lean meat by itself contains almost no calcium, unlike the dog's natural diet which would contain some bone. If prepared foods are used, whether canned, dry or semi-moist, the instructions should be followed carefully.

Another major question is whether a dog should have variety in his diet or if a standard diet is sufficient. There is ample evidence that dogs can live quite satisfactorily and be perfectly healthy for a lifetime on an unvarying diet provided this is complete nutritionally; undoubtedly the dog's wild relatives may at times eat a similar diet for long periods of time. However, this approach to feeding takes no account of the possible pleasures of eating, and there is evidence that dogs do enjoy variety in their diet. It is generally found that most dogs prefer a novel food to a familiar one provided the two are comparably palatable. This suggests that dogs are rather like humans and appreciate variety.

Two of the three main forms of pet foods: dry and semi-moist.

Tinned foods are balanced to provide the correct nutriments.

Showing and breeding

From the long-bodied, short-legged Dachshund, bred for digging, to the huge shaggy rescue dog, the St Bernard, each species of dog has its own characteristics, making Canis familiaris *more varied than any other A dog show such as Cruft's, with dogs of all types and sizes on parade, reveals the great diversity, both genetic and behavioural, of the different breeds.*

Left A Cocker Spaniel with two of her pups. In the case of pedigree dogs such as this, the future size and appearance, as well as the general temperament of the offspring can be anticipated

Emergence of the breeds

The broad groupings of dogs – sheep-herding dogs, hounds, terriers and pet dogs – arose at an early stage in the development of the domestic dog, simply because dogs were used, and therefore bred, for different purposes. Within these major groupings it is possible to trace smaller groups of breeds which are closely related in origin, and to single out particular breeds which have interesting histories.

The majority of modern breeds are comparatively recent in origin, principally because the desire of owners and breeders to show dogs in which the particular characteristics of a breed have been closely defined is a relatively new phenomenon. Prior to this, the appearances of different dogs belonging to the same breeds were much more varied than today. For example, a hundred years ago the German Shepherd dog was not a distinct breed, but instead there were German 'sheepdogs' of varying sizes and colours.

The German Shepherd dog was introduced into the United Kingdom early this century, but after World War I it became known as the Alsatian; it has recently been officially renamed the German Shepherd dog to bring the United Kingdom into line with the rest of the world.

Of existing breeds, the Greyhound and the Saluki can be traced back farthest; very similar dogs were depicted in middle eastern art several thousand years ago. At the other extreme, one of the most modern breeds is the Australian Terrier. This was developed by breeding between various English terriers, including the Yorkshire, Cairn and Dandie Dinmont, and the Australian Silky Terrier, another recent breed. This process began about 100 years ago, but the characteristics of the breed have been firmly fixed only for about 25 years.

In the United States in 1945 the American Cocker Spaniel was given separate breed status from the English Cocker Spaniel. This new breed with its longer, thicker

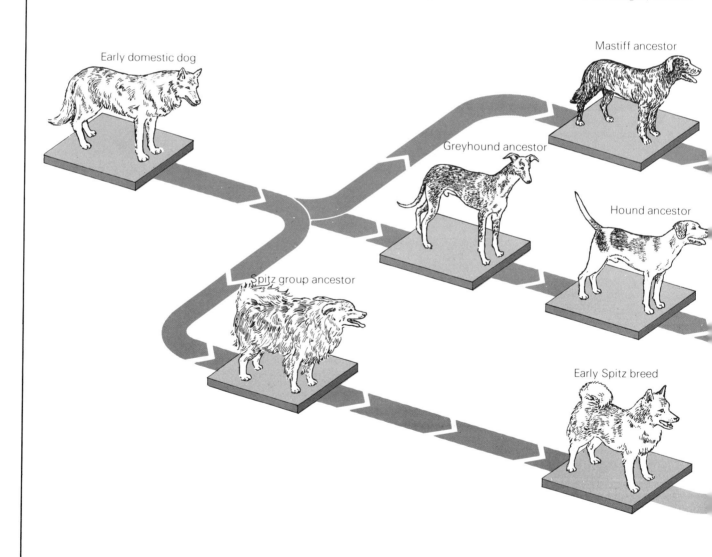

Early domestic dog

Mastiff ancestor

Greyhound ancestor

Hound ancestor

Spitz group ancestor

Early Spitz breed

coat had been selectively bred from English stock. The Spaniel itself is an old breed; the name was used by Chaucer in 1340, and some authorities believe the breed originated in Spain even earlier than that. At that time, the term Spaniel would have included a fairly mixed-looking group of dogs. It is only in comparatively recent times that today's dozen or so Spaniel breeds have emerged, each with a well defined appearance.

Many attempts have been made to create ancestral trees showing the supposed relationships of all the breeds to each other. This is a near impossible job because frequently in the past crossings were made to produce new breeds from quite unrelated dogs. Apart from detailed paintings of a few dogs, it is impossible to say exactly how the ancestors of modern dogs looked, even a few hundred years ago.

Another problem is that there is no international agreement as to how dogs should be grouped for show purposes.

The Spitz group of dogs is split up between at least three other groupings for show purposes in the United States and the United Kingdom. In Sweden, however, where this group is especially strong, they are shown together as a single group in their own right.

In the United States there are six groupings for show purposes: sporting, non-sporting, working, terriers, hounds and toys. In the United Kingdom and Australia there are also six, but they are not the same: working, utility, gundogs, hounds, terriers and toy. On the continent of Europe, there is some variation between countries, but most frequently seven groupings are used: hounds and greyhounds, gundogs, guard and utility dogs, sheepherding dogs, terriers, large companion dogs and small companion dogs. This lack of uniformity reflects the difficulties created by the diverse origins and interrelationships of all the breeds.

The evolution of a breed

Modern breeds of dog, each with their particular physique – body size, limb length, coat type, temperament – differ from their ancestors, whose appearance would have been much more varied. Deliberate cross-breeding by owners and breeders to develop certain characteristics has resulted in the many types today. The diagram, below, gives a graphic illustration of the complexity of one breed's evolution, that of the Staffordshire Bull Terrier.

Early Mastiff

Early Bulldog

Terrier ancestor

Black and Tan Terrier

Bull and Terrier

Staffordshire Bull Terrier

A wide variation

The genetic patterns of pure- and cross-breeding.

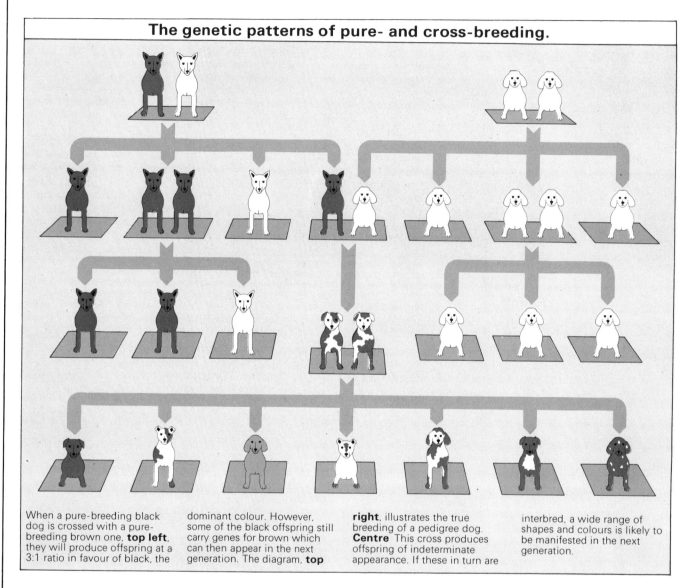

When a pure-breeding black dog is crossed with a pure-breeding brown one, **top left**, they will produce offspring at a 3:1 ratio in favour of black, the dominant colour. However, some of the black offspring still carry genes for brown which can then appear in the next generation. The diagram, **top right**, illustrates the true breeding of a pedigree dog. **Centre** This cross produces offspring of indeterminate appearance. If these in turn are interbred, a wide range of shapes and colours is likely to be manifested in the next generation.

The differences between the many breeds of dog are of great interest genetically, because there is no other species of animal, wild or domesticated, which shows such a high degree of variation. Indeed, if such variations were seen in any wild species, it would almost certainly be concluded that there were in fact several different species, or else that new species were about to develop. However, the fact that all the breeds will produce fertile offspring if crossed shows that the dog is still very much a single species.

The variation within the domestic dog is also surprising because so many different characteristics are affected, for example, coat colour, coat type, body size, limb length, tail shape, head shape, sense of smell and temperament. These characteristics can be shown to be genetically independent of each other. If two breeds with mismatching physical characteristics such as limb length, coat length and head shape are crossed, the first generation will be a mixture roughly halfway between the two parents. If the offspring, which are fairly similar to each other in appearance, are bred together, the members of the next generation will not be uniform in appearance but will be an assortment of, for example, short legs with big bodies, long legs with small bodies, different lengths of upper and lower jaw; they will not necessarily bear any resemblance to either of their grandparents.

The explanation for this is that for some reason the mechanisms that exist in most species to limit the variations within the species seem to have broken down. This has presumably been caused by years of selective breeding for different types of dog. It has been suggested that there may be something special about the dog which has allowed this to happen, because comparable variations have not

The Pekingese, **left**, is a good example of selective breeding by man. Developed in China, the breed did not reach the west until 1860. They symbolized the lions of Buddha, and many households had china 'Fo' dogs like the one pictured above. The two skulls, **below left**, show just how wide the physical variation between domestic dogs can be. The left-hand skull is that of a Golden Retriever, that on the right is a Pekingese.

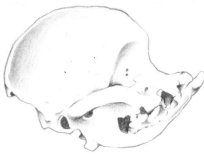

occurred in other domestic species, such as cows and cats. However, the selection of cows has been primarily for milk and meat yield, and not for other characteristics. For cats, a semi-wild population with freedom of choice for mating has always existed. The dog, on the other hand, has been developed by man for innumerable uses and often simply for its appearance. Therefore it may well have been subject to greater selective breeding than any other species.

Because the dog species shows all this variation in appearance and character, the strict control of the breeding of pedigree dogs is sensible. As many present day breeds are relatively recent in origin, their particular characteristics are not necessarily firmly fixed as yet, and therefore any mixing with another breed, or impurely bred dogs, may have an adverse affect on appearance.

Several breeds are derived from a small number of individuals, and in other breeds the major bloodlines are very limited. In either case there can be genetic problems; inherent faults in some members of the breed appear to be passed on from generation to generation through certain individuals. Some authorities believe that infertility, blindness and joint problems can be passed on in these circumstances. The defect can be eliminated by not breeding from affected individuals, but unfortunately faults can sometimes be carried without being displayed physically.

It is difficult to say whether the dog as a species can become any more diverse. Theoretically it probably can, but now that strict standards are laid down for recognized breeds, there is little impetus for the development of new breeds. There is also the view that nature should not be stretched too far, and that the variations existing today are quite sufficient.

Distinctive behaviour

Above Huskies are by nature loyal to one master. **Centre** Some breeds have a natural tendency to guard their own territory, while others inherit an instinct to retrieve, **opposite top right**.
Basenjis, probably developed in isolation, exhibit unique behaviour, **opposite below right**.

The physical differences between dog breeds are clear for all to see, but behaviour differences are more subtle and difficult to define. The Austrian zoologist Konrad Lorenz, in his early writings about the domestic dog, distinguished clearly between two groupings. The first included the northern Spitz dogs, such as the Husky, Spitz, Chow-Chow and Elkhound. Lorenz designated these the 'lupus' type, lupus being the scientific name for the wolf, and suggested that they were much more 'one man' dogs than the members of other breeds. The lupus type are strong in personality, and need a relatively strong character in their master. These dogs will be exceptionally obedient and devoted to such a person, but they will not give the same degree of loyalty to anyone else.

Other dogs, which Lorenz termed the 'aureus' type, using the scientific name for the golden jackal, were said to be less independent and strong-willed, and more ready to serve more than one master. This group makes up the majority of pet dogs. While there is now some doubt about the theory that dogs have both wolf and jackal ancestry,

there is nonetheless a clear distinction between breeds as to whether they will serve more than one master.

One breed whose members have certain behavioural idiosyncrasies is the Basenji, which originated in Africa. These dogs very rarely bark, but they do make all the other sounds common to dogs, and some individuals can be very vocal indeed. Basenjis are much better at climbing than almost any other breed, although, of course, they cannot climb as well as a cat. Another unusual trait is that Basenji bitches come into heat on average only once a year, half as frequently as other breeds; in this they are similar to all the wild species of canids. Taken with the other peculiarities of the breed, this suggests that Basenjis were isolated from other breeds of domestic dog for an extremely long time.

The characteristic behaviour of many breeds is the result of the particular role for which they have been bred. Certain types of Sheepdog, notably the Border Collie, will show an inherent tendency to round up even people, and will try to do this without any special training. Similarly Pointers can readily be trained to point, and Retrievers to

fetch a stick, and carry a newspaper or shopping basket.

While any dog can act as a watchdog, because all dogs have a natural tendency to defend their own territory, some breeds are undoubtedly much more effective in this role than others, and this often reflects their history. These include the breeds of the Spitz group and what are usually called utility breeds such as the Doberman Pinscher and Mastiff; the ancestors of these breeds were frequently used as guard dogs.

The supposedly aggressive nature of certain breeds is difficult to assess because, as has been explained, dogs display many types of aggression. There are no breeds that are naturally aggressive towards people, but a minority of individuals of any breed of dog may attack a human, but almost always only if provoked. The threshold of provocation may be lower in some breeds; the Bull Terrier for example has an aggressive reputation based on its background as a bull baiter. However, any dog of any breed that attacks unprovoked is probably an unstable individual that is best destroyed.

The pedigreed dog

The relative virtues of pedigree and non-pedigree dogs are frequently the subjects of endless, lively discussions. Pedigree dogs have undoubtedly become more popular this century, and on balance it seems worthwhile to have a dog with a known background. In the United Kingdom, for example, pedigree dogs now comprise about half the total number of dogs owned.

One of the commonest arguments in favour of a crossbred or mongrel dog is that it will not be highly strung in the way that some pedigree dogs are said to be. This is based on the assumption that pedigree dogs may be highly inbred, and therefore show some behavioural peculiarities. This might conceivably be the case for some of the uncommon breeds, but is extremely unlikely for the popular ones, where the breeding population is very large. Since behaviour characteristics differ between breeds, it is more possible to predict the character of a purebred dog than that of a crossbred or mongrel.

Mongrels or crossbreds are often given away as 'mistakes', or obtained from animal welfare organizations as strays. In the former instance, the dog will often be a crossbred, where both mother and father were purebred dogs but of different breeds, while in the case of strays, a higher proportion are likely to be mongrels, where three or more breeds have contributed to the ancestry of the dog.

The life saving aspect of giving a good home to a stray mongrel dog or puppy is perhaps the best reason for obtaining this type of dog. Undoubtedly more mongrels are born each year than there are homes available to take them, so on welfare grounds there are excellent reasons to adopt such pets.

While a mongrel will be free, or cost just a modest sum, a pedigree puppy will cost a significant amount of money, which will vary depending on the breed and the quality of the puppy purchased. If the dog is being bought as a pet, the quality of parentage in show terms is of little consequence, because it is only on the showbench, and not in the personality, that such parentage will be reflected.

The main advantage that a pedigree puppy has over a

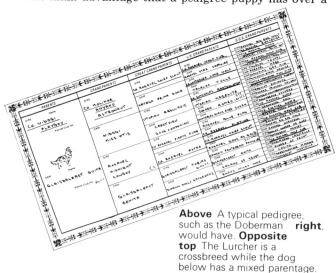

Above A typical pedigree, such as the Doberman **right**, would have. **Opposite top** The Lurcher is a crossbreed while the dog below has a mixed parentage.

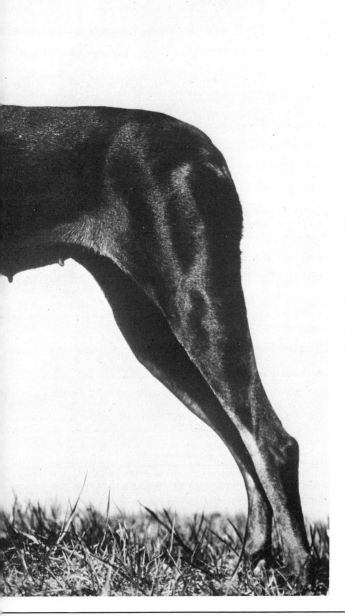

mongrel is that the future appearance and size of the dog, as well as its broad personality, can be anticipated. This is not to say that some mongrels do not look extremely handsome. It is just that they will not conform to a standard type, and their final size cannot be predicted while they are puppies. The pedigree is obviously an advantage if the owner intends to breed dogs at some time. There is generally a ready market for pedigree puppies and, although taking all costs into account, the owner cannot necessarily expect to make a profit, there will at least be some return from the sale of pups.

In most countries there is a registration system for pedigree dogs, whereby a central organization provides certification of pedigree. If a puppy is being bought as a pet it need not be registered, but this should be done if there is any likelihood of breeding from it in the future.

There are a few breeds in some countries, such as the Jack Russell Terrier and the Lurcher in the United Kingdom, which are not recognized by the central dog authority as pedigree dogs. These are sometimes called typed dogs, and may become recognized in the future, as the Border Collie was recently in the United Kingdom and United States.

Dogs on parade

Above Bulldog competition at the Ladies' Kennel Club, Holland Park House, Kensington, in 1896.
Left Measuring a Whippet to see how its size compares with the ideal standard for the breed, at a local French dog show.

The showing of dogs in competition is popular in most countries, but the types of competition vary widely. The commonest type of dog show is a sort of beauty contest, where dogs are judged against each other according to how closely they correspond to an ideal standard for their breed. In some countries, such as the United States, the United Kingdom and Australia, this beauty element is the only, criterion for judging, although dogs can still be dismissed for showing bad temperament. In several countries, especially the European ones, some evidence of working ability is also taken into account.

There are other types of show where dogs are judged specifically on aspects of their working ability. Obedience championships are becoming increasingly popular; dogs are assessed on their abilities at a range of tasks including their response to instructions such as heel, sit, wait and come. Other tests require dogs to demonstrate more specific abilities, for example smell discrimination by picking out a scented cloth from a pile of rags. In other shows, such as sheepdog trials and field trials for gundogs, breed-related working abilities are judged.

While these trials of working ability are becoming more popular, the classical dog show where beauty counts is still the most widespread. Such shows are not run in the same way in all countries, but most have adopted many rules and practices pioneered by the British Kennel Club, which was the first national organization of its kind when it was founded in 1873. The American Kennel Club is now the largest, registering around a million dogs each year. The clubs of continental Europe have national status, but also have an overall controlling body, the Federation Cyno-logique Internationale, which is based in Brussels.

These central clubs organize a range of activities, but most notably they control the registration of pedigree dogs, the breed standards, the procedure at dog shows, and the regulation of awards for winning dogs. They also make special arrangements to encourage beginners, so that they can compete with each other and learn about showing dogs, rather than face competition from champions immediately.

If a dog wins at a major show, it may be awarded champion status for that breed; this will depend on how

Cruft's show: the top dogs

First held in 1886, Cruft's is perhaps the most famous of all dog shows, enjoying royal patronage from Queen Victoria in its early days. The Kennel Club has run the Cruft's show at Olympia since 1948, and the picture, **above**, shows the scale of the event. Entries are now so numerous that dogs must qualify for it by winning prizes at other shows.
Below Coveted medals commemorating Cruft's shows.

often it has won and the type of show in which it has been competing. There is much variation between countries as to exactly how champion status is achieved. If a dog wins best in breed at a show, it will usually go on to compete for best in group, and if it is successful again, for best in show.

Judging is obviously very important for all these competitions, and judges will give either a verbal or written account of the reasons for their choice following the show. In some countries they do this automatically, in others only if asked to do so. The very best dogs are those that win successive shows under a number of different judges.

Index